The Art of Journaling

In "The Art of Journaling: Transforming Thoughts into Actions," readers are invited on a transformative journey that explores the power and simplicity of daily journaling. This insightful guide illuminates the profound impact that a consistent journaling practice can have on personal growth, mental clarity, and emotional resilience. Through a blend of personal anecdotes, psychological research, and practical advice, the book demystifies the process of journaling, making it accessible and engaging for everyone, regardless of their writing experience.

This book is dedicated to breaking down the barriers to journaling, with sections on overcoming writer's block, finding your unique journaling voice, and making journaling a habit that sticks. Practical tips and prompts are scattered throughout, designed to spark creativity, foster self-reflection, and encourage mindfulness.

"The Art of Journaling" also tackles the digital versus paper debate, providing readers with the pros and cons of each and tips on finding the medium that best suits their personal style and goals. Special attention is given to privacy concerns and how to create a safe space for self-expression.

The book culminates in a powerful call to action, encouraging readers to embark on their own journaling journey with confidence and curiosity. With its blend of inspirational stories, practical strategies, and hands-on exercises, "The Art of Journaling: Transforming Thoughts into Action," is an essential guide for anyone looking to deepen their self-understanding, cultivate gratitude, and live a more intentional life.

Contents

Introduction		6
Chapter 1. Getting Started		**8**
1.1	Starting with a Single Line	8
1.2	The Power of Doodling	9
1.3	Writing Letters to Your Future Self	11
1.4	The One-Word Prompt Start	12
1.5	Date and Weather Entries: The Simplest Beginning	14
1.6	Using Stickers and Washi Tape for Inspiration	15
1.7	Creating Borders and Sections	17
1.8	The "What I Did Today" Entry	18
1.9	Mind Mapping Your Thoughts	20
1.10	The Gratitude Log Starter	21
Chapter 2. Elevating Your Journaling Game		**24**
2.1	Bullet Journaling Basics	24
2.2	Sketch and Doodle Journaling	26
2.3	Nature Journaling in Urban Settings	27
2.4	Field Notes for the City Dweller	29
2.5	The Art of Zentangle in Journaling	31
2.6	Mindfulness and Meditation Logs	32
2.7	Dream Diary Entries	34
2.8	Travel Journaling, Even If It's Local	36
2.9	Audio Journaling: An Alternative Approach	37
2.10	Photographic Journaling for the Visual Soul	39

Chapter 3. Making Journaling a Habit — 42

3.1	Setting Realistic Journaling Goals	42
3.2	The Five-Minute Morning Journal	44
3.3	Night Reflections: Ending Your Day on Paper	46
3.4	The Lunch Break Quick Journal	47
3.5	Using Journaling Prompts Effectively	49
3.6	Creating a Dedicated Journaling Space	51
3.7	Journaling with a Partner or Friend	52
3.8	Keeping a Journal at Work	54
3.9	On-the-Go Journaling Solutions	55
3.10	Tracking Progress and Reflecting on Growth	57

Chapter 4. Painting Your Pages with Color — 59

4.1	Emotional Palette	59
4.2	Nature Sketching for the Non-Artist	61
4.3	Writing Poetry in Your Journal	62
4.4	The "Stream of Consciousness" Technique	64
4.5	Playing with Perspective: Sketching the Same Object Multiple Times	65
4.6	Incorporating Mixed Media	67
4.7	The Role of Music in Creative Journaling	69
4.8	Using Quotes as Journaling Prompts	70
4.9	Designing Your Own Journaling Prompts	72
4.10	The Blank Space: Leaving Room for Future Thoughts	73

Chapter 5. The Urban Jungle Notebook — 76

5.1	Urban Nature Spots	76
5.2	Drawing Nature When You Think You Can't	78
5.3	Mindfulness Exercises Outdoors	79
5.4	Crafting Your Portable Nature Journaling Kit	81
5.5	Weather Patterns and Your Mood	83

	5.6	Urban Wildlife Observations	85
	5.7	Plant Growth Tracking	86
	5.8	Nature Journaling as a Group Activity	88
	5.9	Nature's Impact on Personal Growth	89

Chapter 6. Embracing Imperfection in Your Journal — 93

	6.1	Perfection is Not the Goal	93
	6.2	Finding Time to Journal Regularly	94
	6.3	Dealing with Journaling Blocks	96
	6.4	Overcoming Self-Criticism in Artistic Expression	98
	6.5	Journaling During Emotional Times	100
	6.6	Managing Multiple Journals	101
	6.7	Dealing with Distractions and Staying Focused	103
	6.8	Choosing the Right Materials	105
	6.9	Keeping Your Journal Private	106
	6.10	Rekindling Passion for Journaling	108

Chapter 7. Mindful Journaling: Transforming Thoughts into Power — 111

	7.1	Cultivating Positive Narratives	111
	7.2	Journaling Through Anxiety	113
	7.3	Reflective Journaling for Depression	114
	7.4	The Relationship Between Journaling and Sleep	116
	7.5	Emotional Release Techniques	118
	7.6	Gratitude Journaling and Happiness	119
	7.7	Addressing Burnout Through Journaling	121
	7.8	Self-Discovery Prompts	123
	7.9	Setting Intentions and Goals	125
	7.10	Coping Strategies and Journaling	126

Chapter 8. Beautifying Your Journal: The Essential Guide to Layouts — 129

	8.1	Foundation of Visual Journaling	129

	8.2	Incorporating Calligraphy and Hand Lettering	131
	8.3	The Role of Color Psychology	132
	8.4	Stencil Art in Journaling	134
	8.5	Creating Themes for Your Journal	135
	8.6	The Art of Collage in Journal Entries	137
	8.7	Using Nature Elements in Your Journal	139
	8.8	Seasonal Decorations and Motifs	140
	8.9	Personalizing Your Journal Cover	143
	8.10	Organizing Your Journal Aesthetically	145

Chapter 9. Merging Methods for a Masterpiece — 147

	9.1	Synergy of Techniques	147
	9.2	The KonMari Method in Journaling	149
	9.3	Journaling for Career Development	150
	9.4	Advanced Sketching Techniques	152
	9.5	Digital Journaling Tools and Apps	153
	9.6	Creating a Journaling Blog or Vlog	155
	9.7	The Science of Journaling: Research and Studies	157
	9.8	Journaling for Educational Purposes	159
	9.9	Legacy Journaling for Future Generations	160
	9.10	The Philosophy Behind Journaling	162

Conclusion — 165

References — 168

Introduction

Have you ever found yourself at the kitchen table at 2 AM, surrounded by a sea of crumpled paper, an open journal in front of you, and a pen that's just run out of ink? Well, I have. In one of those life-defining, slightly melodramatic moments of mine, I realized that the jumbled mess on my table (and in my head) could actually morph into something resembling clarity and purpose, all thanks to journaling. It wasn't just a mess; it was the beginning of a journey. A journey that, believe it or not, steered my life in a direction I never saw coming. And that's what we're here to talk about.

This book isn't just your run-of-the-mill guide to scribbling down thoughts. No, we're diving into the world of art journaling - a unique blend of creativity and introspection that promises not just to collect your scattered thoughts but to bring them together in a way that makes your purpose in life clearer. It's like having a heart-to-heart with your inner self, but you get to use fancy pens and maybe a bit of glitter.

Now, you might be wondering how we're going to tackle such a vast topic. Fear not, my friend. I've laid out a smorgasbord of journaling goodness for you. We'll start with the basics, easing into the different methods of journaling, then gently nudge you towards incorporating this practice into your daily life. And for those seasoned journaling veterans out there, I've thrown in some advanced techniques to spice up your journaling game. Throughout, you'll find a mix of practical exercises, heartwarming (and sometimes embarrassing) personal stories, and a dollop of scientific research to back up why spilling your guts onto paper is genuinely good for you.

Who is this book for, you ask? It's for anyone and everyone. Whether you're a journaling newbie curious about where to start or a seasoned pro looking to delve deeper into your practice, there's something in here for you. I've written this book to resonate with a wide array of adults, all united by a common goal - to find a bit more clarity and perhaps a splash more color in their lives.

My passion for journaling isn't just about the act itself; it's about what it represents. It's a tool, a friend, a confidant in times of chaos. Writing from a place of authenticity and compassion, I aim to connect with you, dear reader, on a personal level. To inspire you to embark on your own journaling journey, with all its ups and downs.

Drawing upon a wealth of research, including psychological studies and expert opinions, this book isn't just my musings on the magic of journaling. It's grounded in the real, tangible benefits that journaling can have on your mental, emotional, and cognitive well-being.

So, I invite you to approach this book with an open mind and an open heart. Let's explore together how journaling can indeed transform your life, one page at a time. And, before we dive into the nitty-gritty, I want to say a heartfelt thank you. Thank you for joining me on this adventure. Together, let's uncover the joys and challenges of journaling, fostering a sense of camaraderie and mutual support from the get-go. Here's to our shared journey towards self-discovery and personal growth. Let's turn the page and begin, shall we?

Chapter 1

Getting Started

Ever found yourself staring at a blank journal page, the cursor blinking mockingly on an equally barren screen, or the pen hovering hesitantly over paper? It's a common scene for many, akin to a painter facing an untouched canvas or a chef pondering an array of ingredients before the first chop. The initial step often feels insurmountable, not due to a lack of ideas but the overwhelming pressure of beginnings. Yet, what if I told you that all it takes to break through this barrier is as simple as drawing a single line? Yes, a solitary line. No grand gestures, no profound words—just one line. This chapter unpacks the profound simplicity and versatility of starting with a single line, illustrating how such a minimal act can be the gateway to a richer, more fulfilling journaling practice.

1.1 Starting with a Single Line

Simplicity is Key

The act of drawing a single line on a page is disarmingly simple, yet it represents a significant leap over the hurdle of starting. It's a physical manifestation of intent, a declaration that you're ready to engage with your thoughts and the page in front of you. This action mirrors the process of dipping a toe into the water before plunging in; it's a test, an experiment, a whisper to the self that says, "I'm here, and I'm ready to begin." In the realm of journaling, where the blank page symbolizes infinite possibilities and, paradoxically, an intimidating void, the simplicity of a line serves as a gentle initiation into the practice.

Versatility of a Line

Once etched onto the page, this line transcends its initial simplicity. It becomes a foundation, a starting point from which the rest of your entry can blossom. Consider how a single horizon line transforms into a landscape in art—a principle that applies equally to journaling. This line can morph into a border, cradling your words, thoughts, and reflections. It can evolve into shapes, diagrams, or maps that chart your emotional or literal journeys. Its role is as fluid as your needs and creativity demand, serving both as scaffolding for structured entries and a springboard for freeform exploration.

A Line as a Starting Point

Introducing a line onto a page does more than just mark the beginning of your journaling session; it significantly alleviates the pressure of facing a blank slate. There's something about that initial mark that reduces the vastness of the empty page, making the task of filling it seem less daunting. It acts as a beacon, guiding your thoughts and words to flow towards it. This concept isn't just applicable to journaling but is reflected in various creative and professional fields. A chef begins a sophisticated dish with a single chop, a builder lays one brick to start a structure, and similarly, your line is the first brushstroke of what will become a personal masterpiece of insights, reflections, and discoveries.

Metaphorical Significance

The line you draw holds metaphorical weight, symbolizing the first step in a broader voyage towards self-expression and discovery. It's a testament to the courage of beginning, the willingness to confront the unknown, and the commitment to a process of growth. In journaling, each line, word, and entry builds upon the last, contributing to a larger narrative of personal evolution. This line, therefore, is not just a mark on a page but a milestone in your journey. It stands as evidence of your resilience, a reminder that every grand journey begins with the simplest of actions.

Incorporating this understanding into your journaling practice transforms how you approach the blank page. It becomes less about the daunting task of filling space and more about the act of starting, of making that initial, deliberate mark. From there, you're free to explore, to expand, and to express, all stemming from the simplicity and significance of a single line.

As we progress, remember the power inherent in starting small. The line is your ally, your first step, and your foundation. Let it lead you into the depths of your thoughts and the breadth of your imagination.

1.2 The Power of Doodling

Doodling isn't just about scribbling aimlessly on a corner of your page while you're on hold with customer service. It's a lot more than that, especially when it comes to journaling. Have you ever noticed how, when your mind wanders, your pen starts to dance across the page, creating shapes and patterns almost on its own? That's not just killing time; it's a form of meditation. When you let your hand move freely, without directing it too much, you're giving your brain a break. It's like letting your mind take a deep breath. This can be particularly helpful if you're feeling anxious about what to write in your journal. The act of doodling helps clear that mental clutter, making space for more structured thoughts to emerge.

Now, let's talk about the beauty of doodles—they're not supposed to be perfect. This is where you get to throw out all those pesky rules about what constitutes "good art." Doodles are your creative freedom manifesting on paper. They're quirky, spontaneous, and incredibly personal. Ever doodled a series of tiny stars or a string of abstract shapes? That's your creative voice, no judgment needed. This mindset can be incredibly liberating, especially if you've ever felt intimated by the blank page. Doodles are your allies, reminding you that creativity is not about perfection but expression.

Here's where it gets interesting. Those random doodles? They can spark some of your best journaling ideas. Maybe that series of circles becomes a metaphor for the different roles you play in life, or those abstract shapes remind you of a dream you had last night. Suddenly, you're not just doodling; you're uncovering themes and stories to explore in your journal. It's like planting seeds without even realizing it, and then watching in surprise as they sprout into ideas for more structured entries. This is where doodles reveal their secret power—they're not just random drawings; they're the sparks of inspiration that can light up your journaling practice.

Incorporating doodles into your journal isn't just fun; it's a way to enrich your entries and make your journal uniquely yours. Here are a few suggestions on how you can weave doodles into your journaling:

- **Borders and Dividers**: Use doodles to create borders around your pages or divide sections. This not only adds a visual element to your journal but can also help organize your thoughts. A vine of leaves could separate personal reflections from daily to-do lists, for example.
- **Illustrations for Entries**: Got a story about your day? Why not add a small doodle that captures a moment, like the coffee cup from your favorite café or the rain-soaked streets you walked down? These illustrations can bring your words to life and serve as visual anchors for your memories.
- **Backgrounds**: Light, repetitive doodles can serve as a unique background for your journal pages. Think of it as creating your own personalized stationery. Just ensure your doodles are light enough so your writing remains legible.
- **Mood Indicators**: Use specific doodles to indicate your mood for the day. A sunshine doodle for happy days, storm clouds for tougher times, or a simple leaf for days of growth. Over time, you'll create a visual mood tracker within your journal pages.

Remember, the goal here is not to turn you into a professional artist (unless that's your aim, of course) but to enrich your journaling experience. Doodles add layers to your entries, making your journal not just a collection of words but a visual representation of your thoughts, moods, and creativity. So next time you find yourself hesitating over a blank page, let your pen wander and see where it takes you. Who knows what ideas and stories those doodles will unveil?

1.3 Writing Letters to Your Future Self

Imagine sitting down with a cup of your favorite beverage, a pen in hand, and your journal open to a blank page. Instead of the usual entries, today, you're tasked with writing a letter to a very special person: you, but five years from now. This isn't just any letter; it's a bridge across time, a way to connect with the future you with honesty, hope, and perhaps a dash of humor.

Personal Connection

There's something inherently intimate about writing a letter to your future self. It's like whispering secrets into the wind, trusting they'll find their way back to you. This act creates a unique personal connection to your journal. It becomes more than a collection of daily musings or reflections; it transforms into a treasure chest, safeguarding messages to a future you. The emotional significance here can't be understated. It's an acknowledgment that the person you are today has hopes, dreams, and perhaps even warnings for the person you'll become. It's a heart-to-heart with yourself, spanning the years.

Goal Setting

Here's where the rubber meets the road. This letter to your future self is the perfect canvas for setting personal goals or expressing hopes for the future. It's about casting a vision for where you want to be and who you aspire to become. Maybe you hope to have mastered a new skill, achieved a significant professional milestone, or embraced a healthier lifestyle. Writing these goals down in a letter format personalizes them, making them more tangible and real. It's like making a pact with your future self, setting the stage for growth, development, and achievement. Remember, these goals don't have to be monumental; they just need to be meaningful to you.

Reflective Practice

Diving into this exercise, you're embarking on a reflective journey. It forces you to pause and take stock of where you are right now, in this moment. What are your values, your passions, your fears? How do you hope these will evolve over the years? This reflection isn't about judgment or self-criticism. It's an opportunity to acknowledge your current state, celebrate your progress, and gently nudge yourself toward your aspirations. It's about recognizing your strengths and areas for growth, setting a direction for your personal evolution. This reflective practice can be incredibly grounding, offering clarity and motivation to move forward.

Overcoming the Blank Page

For many, the blank page is a daunting adversary. Yet, when you're writing a letter to your future self, the focus shifts. It's no longer about filling the page with perfect prose or insightful reflections. It's about the message, the connection, the intention. This shift in

focus can be liberating. Suddenly, the blank page is a canvas for your hopes, dreams, and words of encouragement. It becomes an open door to the future, inviting you to step through with your words. So, instead of staring down the blank page with apprehension, you approach it with a sense of purpose and anticipation. What message do you want to send to the future? What wisdom or reminders will you thank yourself for? This framing turns the challenge of starting into an exciting opportunity to connect with your future self.

As you pen this letter, consider the following to enrich your message:

- **Be Honest**: Speak from the heart. This letter is for you and you alone, so there's no need to hold back. Be honest about your fears, hopes, and dreams.
- **Be Kind**: Offer words of encouragement and kindness. Remember, the future you will have faced challenges and triumphs you can't foresee. A little kindness can go a long way.
- **Be Specific**: Vague goals and wishes might be forgotten. Be as specific as possible about what you hope to achieve or experience.
- **Be Open**: Allow room for change. The paths to our goals are rarely straight. Acknowledge that the journey is as important as the destination and that it's okay if things evolve differently than planned.

Engaging in this practice, you're not just writing a letter; you're creating a time capsule of your current self, filled with hopes, dreams, and aspirations for the future. It's a testament to the belief in personal growth and the power of setting intentions. And while the future remains unwritten, this letter serves as a beacon, guiding you toward the person you aim to become.

1.4 The One-Word Prompt Start

Sometimes, all it takes is a single word to unlock a flood of thoughts, memories, and emotions. This approach strips down the complexity of beginning to its bare essence, focusing on one word to serve as your muse. It's like having a seed from which a vast, sprawling tree can grow, branching out in unexpected directions. This method not only simplifies the starting process but also opens up a myriad of possibilities for exploration and expression.

Simplicity in Focus

The beauty of this method lies in its simplicity. By concentrating on one word, you sidestep the overwhelming prospect of facing the blank page without direction. It's akin to narrowing down the beam of a spotlight onto a single actor on a stage, making the next steps clear and manageable. This focused approach reduces the pressure to create something grand from the get-go, instead inviting a gentle exploration of where this single word might lead you.

Expanding Ideas

From this solitary word, a universe of ideas can emerge. Let's say your word is "bridge." What images does that conjure up? Perhaps a specific bridge you crossed during a significant moment in your life or the concept of bridging gaps between people or ideas. This word could lead you down paths of personal narrative, reflections on connections you've made, or even broader societal commentary. Here's a simple way to expand your ideas:

- **List Associations**: Jot down everything that comes to mind when you think of your word. No filter, just raw thoughts.
- **Draw Connections**: Look at your list and see how these associations connect to your life, your dreams, or your memories.
- **Explore Through Different Mediums**: Don't limit yourself to writing. Sketch, use photos, or collage to express what the word evokes for you.

Personal Relevance

Choosing a word that resonates with you on a personal level deepens the journaling experience. It could be something reflective of your current mood, a goal you're working towards, or a concept you're grappling with. When a word has personal significance, it acts like a key, unlocking doors to rooms within yourself you might not have explored otherwise. This intimate connection with the prompt ensures that your journaling session is not just an exercise in writing but a meaningful dialogue with yourself.

Versatility and Adaptability

What makes the one-word prompt so powerful is its versatility. It effortlessly adapts to any journaling style. If you lean towards the visual, let the word inspire a drawing or a collage. For those who prefer the written word, it could unfold into a poem, a list, or a stream-of-consciousness entry. The key is to let the word guide you without imposing strict rules on how it should be explored. This freedom allows for a rich, varied journaling practice that can evolve over time, keeping the process fresh and engaging.

By focusing on a single word, you give yourself a manageable starting point, a seed from which your ideas can grow organically. This approach not only simplifies the process of beginning but also enriches your journaling practice, making each entry a unique exploration of thoughts, emotions, and creativity.

1.5   Date and Weather Entries: The Simplest Beginning

In the world of journaling, where the vast landscape of your thoughts and experiences stretches out before you, starting with the date and weather might seem, at first glance, a bit like choosing to walk when you have wings. But, oh, how grounding and enlightening this walk can be. This method, uncomplicated as it is, roots your journaling practice in the here and now, serving as a gentle entry point into the broader realms of reflection and creativity.

Documenting the Day

There's a quiet power in recording the date and weather at the beginning of each journal entry. This ritual, simple though it may be, is your bridge to the present moment—a reminder of where you are in the stream of time and space. It anchors your thoughts, giving them a specific context and setting. Think of it as setting the stage before the main act begins; the backdrop and lighting are just as crucial as the performance itself. This act of marking the date and weather isn't just about record-keeping; it's about acknowledging the day's uniqueness, no matter how routine it might seem.

Observational Skills

Paying attention to the weather does more than just fill space on a page; it hones your observational skills. It encourages you to look out the window or step outside, to really see and feel the day. Is the sky a clear, unbroken blue, or are there clouds rolling in, heavy with rain? Does the air have the crispness of autumn, or is it charged with the warmth of summer? This practice nurtures a deeper mindfulness of your environment, turning what might be a passive observation into an active engagement with the world around you. Over time, you'll find this mindfulness seeping into other areas of your life, turning the mundane into moments of unexpected beauty.

Ease Into Journaling

For anyone staring down a blank page, wondering where to start, jotting down the date and weather is like dipping your toes into the water before the dive. It's a low-pressure way to ease into your journaling session, especially on days when the words feel stuck or your thoughts are tangled. There's no need to search for profound insights or craft perfect sentences. You're just capturing a moment in time, setting the scene for whatever comes next. This simplicity can be incredibly freeing, opening the door to further exploration without the weight of expectations.

Building a Habit

Consistency is the bedrock of any journaling practice, but building that habit takes time and, often, a bit of strategy. Here, the ritual of noting the date and weather shines as a daily touchstone for your practice. It's a small, manageable action that can easily become a habit, acting as the thread that connects your days and entries. Over time, this ritual becomes a natural part of your routine, a moment of pause and reflection that you come to look forward to. And as this habit solidifies, you'll likely find yourself more inclined to delve deeper, to explore further, and to discover the rich tapestry of thoughts, feelings, and ideas waiting to be uncovered in your journal.

In the grand scheme of things, the act of noting the date and weather in your journal is akin to laying the first stone on a path. It's the beginning of a journey, yes, but it's also a step that holds its own intrinsic value. It's a practice that, in its simplicity, offers a multitude of benefits—from grounding and mindfulness to ease of entry and habit formation. So, the next time you open your journal to a blank page, remember that sometimes the simplest beginnings can lead to the most profound discoveries.

1.6 Using Stickers and Washi Tape for Inspiration

The blank page in a journal often feels like a daunting expanse of white space. It's pristine, unblemished, and for many, intimidating. But imagine transforming it with the vibrant colors and textures of stickers and washi tape. Suddenly, the page isn't so intimidating anymore. It becomes a canvas for creativity, a playground for your thoughts and ideas. This section explores how these simple decorative elements can serve as a springboard for your journaling adventure, inviting you to express yourself in new and exciting ways.

Visual Stimuli

Stickers and washi tape, or any decorative tape, Emo bring an element of visual stimulation that text alone cannot achieve. Picture opening your journal to find a page adorned with washi tape borders in geometric patterns or stickers that evoke a sense of calm or happiness. These visuals can spark ideas or emotions, guiding your journaling direction for the day. Maybe a floral sticker reminds you of a recent trip to the botanical gardens, prompting a reflective entry on nature's calming effects. Or perhaps a vibrant washi tape border energizes you, leading to a brainstorming session on future projects. The key is in how these visual cues can unlock memories, dreams, and reflections, making the page less about confronting the void and more about exploring possibilities.

Creative Expression

Incorporating stickers and washi tape into your journaling doesn't just brighten up the pages; it's a form of creative expression. Each choice reflects a part of your personality, your current mood, or your aspirations. For instance, selecting a sticker with a motivational quote for the day's entry could signify a need for encouragement or a desire to motivate yourself. On the other hand, choosing washi tape with a whimsical pattern might reflect a playful mood or a longing for light-heartedness. This process of selection allows you to express yourself before even putting pen to paper, setting the tone for your entry and making your journal a more personalized reflection of who you are.

Starting Point for Journaling

Sometimes, the hardest part of journaling is simply starting. Here's where stickers and washi tape can be particularly useful. Let's say you have a collection of stickers related to travel. Placing one on a blank page could serve as a prompt to write about past travels, dream destinations, or even the concept of life as a journey. Similarly, washi tape with a specific theme—like seasons or holidays—can prompt entries tied to those times of the year, evoking memories or prompting reflections on seasonal changes and their impacts on your life. In this way, these decorative elements provide a tangible starting point for your journaling, acting as prompts that ease you into writing.

Personalizing Your Journal

Above all, the use of stickers and washi tape transforms your journal from a generic notebook into a deeply personal artifact. It's no longer just a place to record thoughts; it becomes an extension of your identity. Every sticker placed, every strip of washi tape applied, turns the pages into a mosaic of moments, feelings, and dreams. It's about adding a layer of personal touch that makes opening your journal feel like coming home—a familiar, welcoming space where you're free to be yourself.

Imagine flipping through your journal at the end of the year. Each page, adorned with these embellishments, tells a story beyond words. The bright sun sticker on a summer day's entry, the reflective silver washi tape bordering a page of new year's resolutions—the decorations serve as milestones, each with its own story and significance. This level of personalization not only makes your journal a joy to return to but also enhances the intimacy of the journaling experience. It's a visual diary, a record of your journey through the year, as told through both words and the artful application of stickers and washi tape.

In embracing these decorative tools, you're doing more than just beautifying your journal. You're creating an environment that invites exploration, reflection, and creativity. The stickers and washi tape become collaborators in your journaling process, offering inspiration and sparking ideas. They transform the blank page from a challenge to an opportunity—a space where your thoughts can flow freely, guided by the visual cues and personal touches that make your journal uniquely yours.

1.7 Creating Borders and Sections

When you open your journal to a fresh page, the emptiness can sometimes feel like too much space to fill. It's like standing at the edge of an open field, not knowing which direction to take your first step. But imagine, for a moment, that this field is crisscrossed with paths, each leading to a different part of a garden. Suddenly, the journey seems less overwhelming, right? This is what drawing borders and creating sections in your journal can do. They serve as pathways that guide your thoughts, making the process of journaling not just manageable, but enjoyable.

Structural Foundation

Think of borders and sections as the architecture of your journal page. Just as a house needs a solid frame to hold its shape, your journal entries benefit from a structural foundation. Drawing lines to create distinct areas on a page can transform it from a daunting blank space into a welcoming environment for your thoughts. These lines don't have to be rigid or straight; they can curve and wander, but they serve as boundaries that confine and define the chaos of ideas waiting to spill out. This structure makes the task of journaling feel less like facing an endless desert and more like navigating a well-mapped city.

Organizing Thoughts

The real magic happens in how these borders and sections help organize your thoughts. Imagine you had a day that was a mix of highs and lows, insights and mundane moments. Trying to capture all of that in a stream of consciousness can be overwhelming, leaving important reflections lost in the mix. By segmenting the page, you create dedicated spaces for different aspects of your day or different types of reflection. Here's how it might look:

- **Top Section**: Dedicated to highlights and achievements of the day.
- **Middle Section**: A space for challenges or low points, turning obstacles into lessons.
- **Bottom Section**: Reserved for insights, ideas, or dreams inspired by the day's events.

This method turns a jumble of experiences into an organized narrative, making it easier to reflect on and learn from each day.

Aesthetic Appeal

Let's not overlook the power of beauty. A journal filled with pages that are visually appealing calls out to be used. The act of creating these layouts, choosing which designs border your musings for the day, becomes an act of creativity in itself. This can be as simple as using a ruler to draw neat lines, or as elaborate as designing intricate patterns that reflect your mood or the theme of your entry. The aesthetic appeal of your journal doesn't just make the process more enjoyable; it can also become a source of inspiration, drawing you back day after day. When your journal is a place of beauty, journaling transforms from a task into a treat.

Flexibility in Format

The true beauty of this approach lies in its flexibility. Your journal is your domain, and the borders and sections you create should reflect your unique needs and style. Here are a few ideas to inspire your layouts, but remember, these are just starting points:

- **Grid Layout:** Perfect for those who love structure. Divide your page into equal squares, each a container for a different thought, moment, or reflection.
- **Radial Layout:** Start with a circle in the center of your page and draw lines outward. Each section created by these lines can represent a different aspect of your life, like spokes on a wheel.
- **Freeform Layout:** Let your intuition guide you. Draw organic shapes and let them form the boundaries of your sections. This layout is ideal for those who view journaling as a free-spirited exploration.

Experiment with these ideas, mix them, match them, turn them on their head. The goal is to find a method that makes your heart sing every time you open your journal. And remember, flexibility isn't just about the layout; it's also about allowing your approach to evolve with you. Maybe a grid layout works for you one month, but the next, you find freedom in the fluidity of freeform shapes. This adaptability ensures that your journaling practice remains vibrant, engaging, and deeply personal.

In essence, creating borders and sections is about carving out spaces for your thoughts to breathe, grow, and take shape. It's about turning the vastness of a blank page into a welcoming landscape of possibilities. Through this structured yet flexible approach, you can navigate the complexities of your thoughts and experiences with ease, turning each journal entry into a journey worth taking.

1.8 The "What I Did Today" Entry

Capturing the essence of your day doesn't always require grand gestures or earth-shattering revelations. Sometimes, it's the quiet moments, the seemingly mundane activities, that paint the most vivid picture of our lives. This is where the "What I Did Today" entry shines as a beacon of simplicity and reflection in the journaling landscape. It's an invitation to pause, to look back at your day with a gentle, curious gaze, and to find beauty and lessons in the ordinary.

Reflective Journaling

At its core, this style of entry is a mirror, reflecting the ebb and flow of daily life. It asks you to consider not just what happened, but how those events unfolded, how they felt, and what stirred within you. Did the morning rush leave you feeling frazzled, or did it energize you? How did the afternoon slump affect your mood or productivity? Even the simple act of recounting these moments encourages a deeper engagement with your experiences, turning routine into reflection.

Simplicity in Detail

The magic of the "What I Did Today" entry lies in its embrace of the small, the overlooked. There's a certain poetry to acknowledging the warmth of the sun on your face during a brief walk, the taste of your lunch, the laughter shared with a friend. These details might seem trivial at first glance, but they're the threads that weave the tapestry of our lives. By focusing on these simple details, your journal becomes a repository of the real, the tangible, and the heartfelt.

Routine Building

Incorporating this entry into your daily routine does more than just fill pages; it builds a bridge to a more mindful, present way of living. Over time, the act of jotting down the day's events becomes second nature, a ritual that bookends your day with introspection and awareness. It's a habit that, once established, offers a consistent touchpoint, a moment of calm in the chaos of everyday life. And as this habit takes root, it naturally encourages a broader engagement with journaling, inviting deeper explorations and more varied entries.

Gratitude and Appreciation

Within the recounting of day-to-day activities, there's a unique opportunity to cultivate gratitude and appreciation. It's easy to overlook the good when we're caught in the whirlwind of life, but taking stock of the day offers a chance to recognize and cherish the positive moments. Maybe it was a kind word from a colleague, a delicious meal you cooked, or simply the fact that you made it through a tough day. Highlighting these moments fosters a mindset of gratitude, shifting the focus from what's lacking to what's abundant in your life.

The "What I Did Today" entry, with its reflective nature and focus on the simple details, not only enriches your journaling practice but also enhances your daily life. It encourages mindfulness, gratitude, and a deeper connection to the present moment, transforming the ordinary into something worth remembering.

1.9   Mind Mapping Your Thoughts

When you're staring at a blank page, sometimes linear notes or streams of consciousness don't quite cut it. That's where mind mapping comes in, a dynamic technique that throws the traditional rules of organization out the window. Instead of a start-to-finish approach, mind mapping sprawls in all directions, connecting related ideas through branches that extend from a central concept. It's kind of like watching a tree grow in fast-forward, each branch reaching out to capture sunlight, or in this case, the lightbulb moments of your brain.

Organizing Ideas

The beauty of a mind map lies in its ability to visually organize thoughts in a way that mirrors the natural associative processes of the human brain. Picture this: At the center of your page, you write a word or phrase that's been circling in your mind. From there, you draw lines outward, each leading to a different idea, thought, or question related to that central concept. It's a method that encourages you not to just think outside the box but to forget the box altogether. The result? A page filled with a web of interconnected thoughts, making sense of the chaos in your head. This visual network helps you see relationships between ideas, identify areas that need more exploration, and even spot gaps in your thinking.

Creative Brainstorming

For those moments when the muse seems to have taken a long vacation, a mind map can serve as a creative catalyst. Let's say you're struggling to come up with topics for your journal entries. Start with the word "memories" at the center of your map. From there, branches could lead to "childhood," "travel," "challenges," and "milestones." Before you know it, each of these branches sprouts its own set of sub-branches, filled with specific memories or themes you can dive into. This organic expansion of ideas can turn a vague notion into a rich tapestry of potential entries, ensuring you're never at a loss for words.

Clarity and Focus

Beyond brainstorming, mind mapping can be an invaluable tool for gaining clarity on personal goals, feelings, or challenges. Sometimes, the things we grapple with are complex, tangled in layers of emotion and thought that are hard to unravel. By placing a goal or challenge at the center of your map, you can start teasing out these layers, drawing branches that represent different aspects or factors of the issue. This process not only helps in breaking down complex feelings into manageable pieces but also shines a light on possible paths forward, making the intangible tangible and the overwhelming manageable.

Versatile Application

What sets mind mapping apart is its adaptability across different journaling styles. It's not just for planning or brainstorming; it can transform the way you reflect on your day, dream about the future, or even work through creative projects. Here are a few ways you might use mind maps in your journal:

- **For Reflection**: Place an event or interaction at the center, and use branches to explore your reactions, feelings, and the lessons learned. This can offer insights into your emotional responses and personal growth.

- **For Dreaming**: Center your map around a dream or aspiration. Use the branches to map out the steps you need to take to achieve it, potential obstacles, and resources or support you might need. This turns vague dreams into actionable plans.

- **For Creative Projects**: If you're working on a creative piece, be it a story, a piece of art, or a personal project, a mind map can help you organize your ideas, themes, characters, or visual elements in a way that linear notes cannot.

The versatility of mind mapping ensures that it can be a powerful tool in your journaling arsenal, regardless of your goals or style. It invites you to explore the full spectrum of your thoughts and creativity, turning the daunting blank page into a vibrant canvas of possibilities.

In a world where we often find ourselves overwhelmed by the volume and complexity of our thoughts, mind mapping offers a way to navigate through the noise. It's a technique that encourages exploration, creativity, and clarity, making it not just a tool for journaling but a method for understanding the intricate landscape of our minds. So next time you find yourself at a loss for where to start, or if you're looking to deepen your journaling practice, consider reaching for a pen and letting your thoughts branch out in all directions. The connections and insights you discover might just surprise you.

1.10 The Gratitude Log Starter

In a fast-paced world where we often focus on what's missing rather than what we have, introducing gratitude into our daily routine can be a game-changer. This is where the concept of a gratitude log comes into play, tapping into positive psychology to boost our overall sense of well-being. It's about shifting the lens through which we view our day-to-day life, focusing on the abundance rather than the lack, the joy amidst the chaos.

Gratitude logging isn't about grand gestures or life-altering events; it's about finding value in the small, everyday moments. It could be as simple as a warm cup of coffee in the morning, a call from an old friend, or the comfort of your favorite chair at the end of a long day. These entries serve as gentle reminders of the good that surrounds us, often going unnoticed.

To get started, let's break it down into manageable steps:

- **Start Small**: Begin with just one thing you're grateful for each day. It doesn't have to be profound; what matters is that it's genuine.
- **Be Consistent**: Try to make your entry at the same time each day, creating a ritual. Perhaps it's the first thing you do in the morning or the last thing at night.
- **Use Prompts**: If you're struggling to think of something, use prompts. "What made me smile today?" or "Who made my day better, and how?"

As your gratitude log grows, you may find yourself naturally looking for moments of gratitude throughout your day, knowing you'll be jotting them down later. This anticipation can shift your mindset, making you more attuned to the positive aspects of your life.

To deepen your gratitude practice, consider not just what you're grateful for, but why. This extra step can transform a simple list into a profound exploration of your values, relationships, and what truly brings you joy. For example, if you're grateful for a peaceful morning walk, delve into why it was meaningful. Was it the tranquility, the connection with nature, or perhaps the feeling of taking care of your health? Understanding the "why" adds depth to your entries, turning them into a powerful reflection of your inner landscape.

Here's how you can cultivate this positive habit further:

- **Reflect Monthly**: At the end of each month, look back through your entries. You'll likely notice patterns—things that consistently bring you joy and gratitude. This reflection can be incredibly eye-opening, offering insights into what to prioritize or seek out in your life.
- **Share Your Gratitude**: Occasionally, share your gratitude with others. If a person is the reason for your gratitude, let them know. This not only spreads positivity but also strengthens your relationships.
- **Expand Your View**: As you become more comfortable with the practice, challenge yourself to find gratitude in unexpected places, even in challenges or difficult times. This perspective can be transformative, turning obstacles into opportunities for growth and deepening your sense of gratitude.

The beauty of a gratitude log lies in its simplicity and the profound impact it can have on your outlook on life. By regularly acknowledging and appreciating the good, you're training your brain to focus on positive aspects, fostering a sense of contentment and happiness. This habit, once cultivated, becomes a natural part of your daily routine, a source of light on even the darkest days.

The practice of keeping a gratitude log is more than just a journaling exercise; it's a commitment to recognizing the beauty in the ordinary, the silver linings in every cloud, and the countless blessings that fill our lives, often in disguise. It's a journey towards a more fulfilled, joyful existence, grounded in an appreciation for the here and now.

So, as you move forward with your journaling, consider the gratitude log not just as another entry, but as a tool for transformation. Let it be a daily reminder of the good that surrounds you, waiting to be acknowledged, cherished, and celebrated. With each entry, you're not only filling pages in a journal; you're filling your life with a deeper sense of gratitude and well-being.

Chapter 2

Elevating Your Journaling Game

Imagine stepping into a candy store. Everywhere you look, there's a rainbow of options, each promising a unique flavor adventure. That's kind of what exploring advanced journaling techniques feels like. It's about discovering new ways to express yourself, to capture the moments that matter in vibrant, dynamic ways. This chapter is your guide through this candy store of possibilities, starting with a technique that's as structured as it is liberating: bullet journaling.

2.1 Bullet Journaling Basics

Bullet journaling. You've probably heard the term tossed around in productivity circles or seen the hashtag lighting up Instagram feeds. But what is it, really? It's a customizable organization system but calling it just that is like saying a Swiss Army knife is just a blade. Let's break it down.

Structured Creativity

At its heart, bullet journaling is a blend of organization and self-expression. It's the framework you choose when you want to keep track of your to-dos, but with room to breathe creatively. Imagine planning your week not just with lists, but with sketches of your goals, colorful markers highlighting your priorities, and little doodles that make you smile. It's about turning the mundane into something engaging, transforming what could be a dry list of tasks into a page that motivates and inspires you.

Customization is Key

The beauty of a bullet journal lies in its flexibility. Here, you're the architect, designing a system that mirrors your needs and lifestyle. Do you thrive on detailed daily logs, or are you a big-picture kind of person who prefers monthly overviews? Your bullet journal adapts to you. For those who love to track habits or moods, collections become your best friend, offering a snapshot of your journey toward personal goals. It's like having a personal assistant tailored exactly to your specifications, without the hefty price tag.

Rapid Logging

Bullet journals are known for their unique approach to capturing information, dubbed "rapid logging". This method is all about efficiency, using symbols to categorize entries into tasks, events, or notes at a glance. Picture this: a small dot for tasks, a circle for events, and a dash for notes. It's shorthand that keeps your pages uncluttered and your mind clear. When you review your day or plan the next, these symbols help you quickly assess what's on your plate, what deserves a victory dance, and what insights you've gleaned.

Modules and Collections

Diving deeper, bullet journals are structured around modules: the index, future log, monthly log, and daily log. Think of these as the foundation of your journal, each serving a specific purpose in helping you navigate through time. The index is your table of contents, guiding you through your journal. The future log is where you dream big, jotting down events or goals for the coming months. Monthly and daily logs then break down these aspirations into actionable steps.

But the magic doesn't stop there. Collections are themed pages where you can track, well, anything your heart desires. From books you want to read to workout progress, these collections turn your bullet journal into a living archive of your interests and achievements. It's like having a personal blog in the palm of your hand, but with the intimacy and tangibility that only pen and paper can provide.

Imagine you're planning a trip. In your bullet journal, you could have a collection dedicated to this adventure. One page lists out places to visit, another tracks your saving goals, while a third could be a packing checklist. This way, your journal becomes a central hub for all things related to your trip, turning planning from a task into an exciting part of the journey itself.

Bullet journaling is more than just a method of organization; it's a tool for mindful living, a canvas for personal expression, and a testament to the power of pen and paper in our digital age. Whether you're a meticulous planner or a creative soul searching for structure, bullet journaling offers a path to clarity, purpose, and, most importantly, a touch of joy in the everyday. So, grab a notebook and a pen, and let's start this adventure, one bullet point at a time.

2.2 Sketch and Doodle Journaling

Picture this: your journal, a place where words meet visuals, where your day's chaos finds peace in the strokes of a pen or the brush of a marker. This is sketch and doodle journaling—a method not confined by the boundaries of traditional writing but one that flourishes in the freedom of visual expression. It's where your experiences, thoughts, and even dreams take on a form that's as unique as you are.

Visual Thinking

Visual thinking through sketching and doodling is a transformative way to explore ideas beyond the linear confines of text. It's about letting your thoughts flow in a direction guided by the curve of a line or the shade of a pencil. This method taps into a different part of your brain, encouraging connections and insights that might remain elusive in words alone. Imagine capturing the essence of a quiet morning not with sentences, but with a simple sketch of the sun peeking through your window, its rays casting long shadows across the room. This visual note can evoke emotions and memories in a way that words might not fully capture.

No Artistic Skills Required

Here's the liberating truth: sketch and doodle journaling doesn't demand you to be an artist. Far from it. This practice is about expression and exploration, not perfection. Your doodles and sketches are personal—visual whispers of your day, your mood, your dreams. They don't need to be gallery-worthy; they just need to be yours. So, let go of the self-judgment. A doodle of your cat, a sketch of a coffee cup, abstract shapes that mirror your mood—it's all valid, all valuable. It's about the joy of creation, the act of making marks on a page that reflect your inner world.

Integrating Text and Images

Combining text and imagery opens up new dimensions in your journaling practice. It's about creating a dialogue between what you see and what you feel, between your experiences and your reflections. Here are a few ways to weave together words and visuals:

- Write a brief reflection and then sketch something that symbolizes the main emotion or event from your entry.
- Use doodles as bullet points for your to-do list or goals.
- Sketch a scene from your day and caption it with a memorable quote or conversation.

This blend enriches your journal, making it a multifaceted record of your life. It also allows you to engage with your entries on multiple levels, enhancing recall and deepening understanding.

Tools and Techniques

Diving into sketch and doodle journaling invites you to play with a variety of tools and techniques. Here's a taste of what you could explore:

- **Pens and Markers**: Experiment with different thicknesses and colors. Fine liners are great for detail work, while brush pens add flair to your headers and doodles.
- **Watercolors**: Perfect for adding a wash of color to your pages. They can bring a dreamy quality to your sketches or backgrounds.
- **Shadowing and Contouring**: Add depth to your doodles with simple shadowing techniques. Use a lighter touch on one side and darken the edges or areas furthest from your imagined light source for a 3D effect.
- **Stencils and Stamps**: Not confident in your freehand skills? Stencils and stamps can help structure your visuals while still leaving room for customization and creativity.

These tools and techniques are not just about decorating your pages; they're about discovering new ways to capture and reflect on your life. They encourage you to see your journal not just as a repository of thoughts but as a canvas for your creativity.

In the realm of journaling, sketch and doodle journaling stands out as a vibrant, dynamic method of capturing the world as you see and experience it. It's a tactile reminder of the moments, big and small, that shape your days. This approach doesn't just preserve memories; it invites you to interact with them, to see your life through a lens that's as colorful, complex, and nuanced as the sketches and doodles that fill your pages.

2.3 Nature Journaling in Urban Settings

In the concrete jungle, where nature seems to play hide and seek amid the skyscrapers and sidewalks, finding a green sanctuary might feel like a quest for the elusive. Yet, nature thrives in the urban sprawl, waiting in pocket parks, on windowsills adorned with potted plants, and in the unexpected corners where wildflowers dare to grow. This section is about uncovering these hidden gems and documenting them in your journal, turning the cityscape into a canvas for nature journaling.

Finding Nature Anywhere

The quest for nature in the city is akin to a treasure hunt. It's there, in the veins of the leaves in the park, the moss growing in the cracks of a wall, and the clouds overhead, framed by rooftops. It's in the sparrows bathing in puddles and the trees that line the streets, steadfast in their urban growth. Your journal becomes the map to these treasures. Start by:

- Keeping a lookout for green spaces, no matter how small. Even a single tree can be a subject for your journal.
- Noticing the plants and flowers in your neighborhood. Someone's garden or a community garden can offer inspiration.
- Observing the sky from your window. The changing colors at sunset, the patterns of the clouds, or the phases of the moon are all worthy entries.

Observational Skills

Nature journaling sharpens your senses, turning every outing into an opportunity for discovery. It's about more than just seeing; it's about observing— noting the way light filters through leaves, the sound of birdsong amidst traffic, or the smell of rain on concrete. These observations enrich your journal and deepen your connection to your surroundings. They encourage you to:

- Slow down and really look at what's around you, discovering the beauty in the mundane.
- Use all your senses to experience nature. How does the air smell after it rains? What's the texture of the bark on the trees in your street?
- Record these observations in your journal, using words, sketches, or even collected items like leaves or flower petals (if it's sustainable to do so).

Documenting Change

The city's nature is not static; it shifts with the seasons, telling a story of time and transformation. Your journal can capture this narrative, documenting the subtle and overt changes that occur. From the first buds of spring pushing through the soil to the stark beauty of bare trees in winter, these cycles of growth and dormancy offer a wealth of material for your pages. Consider:

- Making regular visits to the same spot and noting the changes. This could be a park, a garden, or any green space.
- Tracking the progress of a particular tree or plant. How does it change throughout the year?
- Recording weather patterns and their impact on urban nature. How does a summer storm affect the city's flora and fauna?

Mindfulness and Connection

Perhaps the most profound aspect of nature journaling in an urban setting is the mindfulness it cultivates. It's a practice that invites stillness amid the hustle, a momentary pause to breathe and connect. This connection is not just with the environment but with yourself. It's a reminder that nature, with all its cycles and rhythms, is a mirror to our own inner landscapes. To foster this mindfulness:

- Dedicate a few minutes of your journaling time to simply being in the moment, fully immersed in your surroundings.
- Reflect on how the piece of nature you're observing makes you feel. Is there a sense of calm, a spark of joy, or perhaps a nostalgia it evokes?
- Use your journal to explore these feelings, diving into how nature's resilience and beauty resonate with your personal journey.

Nature journaling in an urban environment is an exploration of contrasts and a celebration of finding the wild in the midst of the structure. It's a practice that not only enhances your awareness of the natural world but also enriches your understanding of how you interact with and fit into this urban ecosystem. Whether it's the dandelions growing through cracks in the sidewalk or the canopy of trees that grace the city park, there's a story waiting to be told, a piece of nature ready to be discovered and cherished in your journal.

2.4 Field Notes for the City Dweller

Diving into the heart of urban exploration, imagine transforming your journal into a dynamic tapestry that captures the vibrant, ever-changing tapestry of city life. Field notes for the city dweller aren't just about jotting down what you see; they're an immersive exercise in documenting the pulsating energy, the hidden nooks, and the cultural heartbeat of your urban environment. It's about peeling back the layers of the city, one observation at a time, to reveal a narrative as diverse and dynamic as the streets themselves.

Urban Exploration

The city, with its towering structures and bustling streets, might seem an unlikely muse for journaling. Yet, within its concrete veins flows a rich narrative waiting to be captured. Urban exploration through field notes is your passport to discovering this narrative, offering a fresh perspective on familiar surroundings. Start with a simple walk, but this time, move with the intention of observing, not just passing through. Notice the architectural styles that stand shoulder to shoulder, the graffiti that whispers the city's secrets, and the street vendors that paint the sidewalks with colors and scents. Your journal becomes a living document of these explorations, a place where the city's story unfolds through your eyes.

Sensory Observations

To truly capture the essence of urban environments, engage all your senses in the observation process. The city is a symphony of sounds, from the melody of street musicians to the rhythm of footsteps on pavements. It's a canvas of textures, from the smoothness of glass facades to the roughness of brick walls. And it's an amalgamation of scents, from the inviting aroma of street food to the unexpected fragrance of flowers in a park. Documenting these sensory experiences adds depth to your field notes, painting a vivid picture of urban life that engages not just the mind but the soul. Consider:

- **Listening** to the sounds that define different parts of the city and describing their impact on the urban atmosphere.
- **Touching** surfaces as you pass them, noting the interplay of textures.
- **Smelling** the air in various locales, identifying scents that evoke particular feelings or memories.

Cultural Immersion

Cities are melting pots of cultures, each neighborhood offering a window into a different world. Field notes can serve as a record of these cultural experiences, capturing the diversity that makes urban life so rich and complex. Attend local festivals, visit museums, dine at neighborhood eateries, and immerse yourself in the rituals that define the city's various communities. Reflect on these experiences in your journal, noting not just the events themselves but your reactions and reflections. How do these cultural encounters shape your understanding of the city? How do they influence your sense of belonging or your perspective on diversity? These entries become more than just observations; they're a dialogue with the city and its myriad inhabitants.

Sketches and Maps

While words can capture the essence of your urban explorations, integrating sketches and maps can elevate your field notes, adding a visual dimension that complements your written observations. Sketches don't have to be detailed or artistically refined; they can be quick doodles that capture the shape of a building, the layout of a street, or the profile of a passerby. Maps, on the other hand, can document your journeys through the city, tracing the routes you've taken and marking spots that hold particular significance. These visual elements serve multiple purposes:

- **Enhancing recall** by providing visual cues that trigger memories of places and experiences.
- **Adding a personal touch** to your journal, making it uniquely yours.
- **Encouraging creativity** by inviting you to experiment with different styles and mediums.

Incorporating sketches and maps into your journal turns it into a multidimensional record of your urban adventures, one that captures not just the sights but the essence of city life.

Through the lens of field notes, the city reveals itself not just as a backdrop to our lives but as a character in its own right, with stories to tell and secrets to share. This method of journaling invites you to become an urban explorer, to see the city with fresh eyes, and to document its many facets in a way that is both personal and profound. It's an ongoing conversation with the place you call home, a way to connect with its rhythm, its people, and its culture. So, grab your journal and step out into the city. Adventure awaits on every corner, and every observation is a thread in the vibrant tapestry of urban life.

2.5 The Art of Zentangle in Journaling

In a world where every tick of the clock pressures us to move faster, to do more, there exists a quiet haven within the pages of our journals, a space where time slows down, and the mind finds peace. This haven is often furnished with the art of Zentangle, a practice that marries the joy of drawing with the serenity of meditation. Imagine each stroke of the pen, each curve, and line, not as mere marks on paper, but as a pathway to tranquility, a dance of pen and ink that quiets the mind and centers the soul.

Meditative Drawing

Zentangle isn't just drawing; it's a form of meditation. Picture yourself sitting with your journal, pen in hand, with no end goal but to let the pen glide across the page, creating patterns that grow organically, without premeditation. This process, focusing solely on each stroke, allows the clamor of the outside world to fade away, silencing the chatter of the mind and ushering in a state of calm focus. The repetitive nature of Zentangle patterns, known as "tangles," acts as a mantra of sorts, guiding the practitioner into a meditative state where stress levels drop, and creativity flows unimpeded.

Creativity Without Constraints

One of Zentangle's most liberating aspects is its declaration that there are no mistakes, only opportunities. This philosophy nurtures creativity by removing the fear of failure. Whether you consider yourself an artist or someone who struggles to draw a straight line, Zentangle welcomes you. It doesn't ask for inherent artistic skills; rather, it unfolds from the belief that everyone can create, and through creation, find joy. The focus is on the process, not the product, allowing for a kind of creative freedom that is both rare and profoundly therapeutic.

Integrating Patterns

Incorporating Zentangle patterns into your journal pages can transform them from blank spaces to works of art that capture your mental state, emotions, or simply the whimsy of your imagination. Here's how you can weave Zentangle into your journaling:

- **Borders:** A Zentangle border can turn a page into a framed masterpiece, setting a mood or theme for your written entries.
- **Fillers:** Use tangles as fillers for empty spaces, turning gaps into visual delights that add depth and texture to your pages.
- **Backgrounds:** Faint Zentangle patterns in the background can add a layer of complexity and interest, making your journal a visual as well as a written record of your journey.

These patterns aren't just decorative; they enhance the meditative quality of your journaling, making each page a mindful exploration of both thought and form.

Combining with Text

Blending Zentangle with written entries opens up new avenues for expression. Here are a few ways to marry text with tangles:

- **Framing Text:** Surround a poignant quote or a personal mantra with Zentangle designs, highlighting its significance and making it a focal point of your page.
- **Illustrative Lettering:** Incorporate tangles into the letters of a word or phrase, turning the text itself into a piece of art that echoes the sentiments of your entry.
- **Visual Metaphor:** Use Zentangle patterns to visually represent emotions or concepts discussed in your text, creating a seamless blend of visual and verbal storytelling.

This synthesis of word and image deepens the journaling experience, offering a multisensory reflection on the themes and emotions that percolate through your life.

In the embrace of Zentangle, journaling becomes more than a record of days; it transforms into a sanctuary of calm and creativity, a place where the mind can wander freely, unencumbered by the demands of perfection or the expectations of outcome.

This practice invites you to slow down, to savor each moment and each mark on the page, finding within the tangles a reflection of the intricate, beautiful, and sometimes complex patterns of your inner world. Through Zentangle, your journal becomes not just a keeper of memories but a canvas for the soul, a testament to the quiet power of drawing your way to mindfulness and peace.

2.6 Mindfulness and Meditation Logs

In the tapestry of life, where each thread intertwines with countless others, carving out moments for mindfulness and meditation can feel like finding a quiet clearing in a bustling forest. Your journal, a faithful companion through the ebbs and flows of daily existence, offers a serene space to anchor these practices. Here, amidst the hustle, we discover tranquility, documenting our journey towards inner peace and heightened awareness.

Tracking Mindfulness Practices

Imagine your journal as a garden where seeds of mindfulness are sown. Each entry, a meticulous record of your meditation practices, blossoms into a personal oasis of tranquility. Begin by noting the techniques that resonate with you, whether it's focused breathing, guided imagery, or a quiet walk in nature. Include the duration of each session, as this can reveal patterns over time, shedding light on what practices yield the deepest sense of calm.

Reflections on these experiences, captured in your journal, transform mere logs into a map guiding you towards mindfulness mastery.

- Create a dedicated section for these logs, perhaps marked with symbols or in a specific color, to distinguish them from your regular entries.
- Note the time of day for each practice, as this can help identify when you're most receptive to mindfulness exercises.

Reflecting on Inner Experiences

Within the sanctuary of your journal, reflections on the inner workings of your mind offer profound insights. After each session, take a moment to jot down the thoughts that drifted through your consciousness, the emotions that ebbed and flowed, and any insights that surfaced. This practice isn't about judgment but about observation and acceptance. Over time, these reflections build a bridge to understanding the complex landscape of your inner self, illuminating paths to tranquility and self-awareness.

- Use prompts like "Today, my mind wandered to..." or "The emotion that surfaced most strongly was..." to initiate reflection.
- Consider drawing a mood or emotion wheel in your journal, using colors or symbols to represent different states experienced during meditation.

Incorporating Mindful Prompts

Sprinkle your journal with mindful prompts, invitations to dive deeper into the waters of self-discovery. These prompts, strategically placed among your entries, beckon you to pause, reflect, and engage with the present moment on a profound level. Whether it's contemplating the sensation of the air on your skin or the last time you felt truly alive, these prompts serve as gateways to introspection, fostering a habit of mindfulness that permeates beyond the pages of your journal.

- Examples of prompts include "A moment today I wish I could relive..." or "Something I noticed for the first time today was..."
- Allocate space in your journal for spontaneous responses to these prompts, allowing your reflections to flow freely and without constraint.

Gratitude and Awareness

At the heart of mindfulness lies gratitude, a recognition of the myriad blessings, both grand and minute, that lace our lives. Dedicate pages within your journal to log these moments of gratitude, noting the everyday miracles that often go unnoticed. This practice not only cultivates a deeper connection to the present but also weaves a tapestry of positivity and appreciation that can uplift you in times of turmoil. Through the lens of gratitude, the world unveils itself in a new light, one brimming with wonder and possibility.

- Begin or end each day with a gratitude entry, listing three things you're thankful for, no matter how small.
- Pair each item of gratitude with a brief explanation, deepening the connection between appreciation and awareness.

In the realm of your journal, mindfulness and meditation logs stand as beacons of light, guiding you through the tumult of life towards a haven of peace and introspection. Here, among the whispered reflections and the chronicled journeys of the mind, you discover not just the art of presence but the heart of existence itself. Through diligent tracking, reflective exploration, mindful prompts, and the cultivation of gratitude, your journal transforms into a sanctuary of awareness, a testament to the transformative power of mindfulness in the tapestry of daily life.

2.7 Dream Diary Entries

In the quiet hours of the night, our subconscious mind crafts stories, weaving together symbols, fears, aspirations, and memories into the tapestry of our dreams. These narratives, often dismissed by the morning light, hold keys to understanding our deeper selves. A dream diary, therefore, becomes a precious tool, a gateway into the labyrinth of the subconscious, inviting us to record and explore the rich, sometimes bewildering, landscape of our dreams.

Recording the Subconscious

Initiating a practice of keeping a dream diary involves more than just jotting down what you remember upon waking. It's an act of attentiveness, of learning to listen to the whispers of your subconscious mind. The first step is simple—keep your journal and a pen within easy reach of your bed, primed for use the moment you awaken. As dreams tend to fade quickly from memory, it's crucial to capture them as swiftly as possible. Write down everything you recall; no detail is too small or too mundane. Over time, you'll notice your recall improving, with more of your dreams preserved in vivid detail on the pages of your diary.

- Use bullet points for quick, immediate recollections, then expand on these initial notes to flesh out the narrative of your dream.
- Include emotions, colors, and sensations, as these often carry significant symbolic weight.

Interpretation and Analysis

The process of interpreting dreams is akin to deciphering a personal code, one where symbols and scenarios are imbued with unique meanings. Begin by looking for patterns or recurring themes in your dreams. Do certain symbols or situations appear repeatedly? These could reflect ongoing concerns, unresolved issues, or deep-seated desires in your waking life. Consider the emotions each dream evokes—fear, joy, frustration—and how these might relate to your current circumstances or state of mind.

- Create a "symbol glossary" in your dream diary, noting your personal interpretations of common symbols in your dreams.
- Reflect on how the themes of your dreams might offer insights into your waking life, writing down any revelations or connections you discover.

Creative Inspiration

Dreams are a wellspring of creativity, offering images, narratives, and ideas unfettered by the constraints of logic or societal norms. Many artists, writers, and innovators have drawn upon their dreams for inspiration, finding within them the seeds of stories, artworks, and inventions. Look at your dream diary not just as a record but as a muse, a source of creative raw material that can spark new projects or add depth to ongoing ones.

- Highlight or tag entries that stir your imagination, earmarking them for creative exploration.
- Experiment with translating a vivid dream into a short story, a piece of art, or the basis for a personal essay, letting the dream guide your creative process.

Nightly Routine

Establishing a routine conducive to both remembering and recording dreams is essential. This might involve winding down before bed in a way that primes your mind for vivid dreaming and easy recall. Avoid screens and stimulating activities right before sleep, opting instead for calming rituals like reading, gentle stretching, or meditation. Setting a clear intention to remember your dreams before you drift off can also be surprisingly effective.

- Keep your dream diary and pen by your bed, ready for immediate use upon waking.
- Practice waking slowly, keeping your eyes closed as you recall your dreams before reaching for your diary.

In nurturing the practice of keeping a dream diary, you're doing more than just collecting the ephemeral narratives of the night. You're engaging in a dialogue with your subconscious, exploring the depths of your inner world, and tapping into a well of creativity that knows no bounds. Through the act of recording, interpreting, and drawing inspiration from your dreams, you transform them from fleeting shadows into illuminating guides, shining a light on the path to self-discovery and creative fulfillment.

2.8 Travel Journaling, Even If It's Local

The world around us is a tapestry of stories, waiting patiently for us to thread our own narratives into its vast expanse. Travel journaling, in essence, isn't confined to the realms of distant lands or exotic locales; it's an art form that celebrates exploration in all forms. From the cobblestone streets of your hometown to the hidden gems just a day's trip away, every journey offers a treasure trove of experiences ripe for journaling.

Adventures Near and Far

The misconception that travel journaling requires passports and plane tickets is one we're setting aside. The spirit of adventure isn't measured in miles but in the willingness to see the familiar through a lens of curiosity and wonder. Your local park, a new neighborhood café, or a nearby town all hold within them the essence of discovery. This approach to travel journaling invites you to document life's adventures, regardless of their geographical scope. It's about capturing the essence of movement, the joy of stumbling upon the unexpected right around the corner.

- Start with a place within walking distance and pretend you're seeing it for the first time. What details emerge?
- Plan a "tourist day" in your own city, visiting landmarks or museums you've never been to before.

Capturing Experiences

The heart of travel journaling lies in capturing the moments that resonate, threading together narratives that bring your experiences to life. Whether it's a sketch of a bustling street corner, a snippet of conversation overheard in a café, or a ticket stub from a local museum, these artifacts serve as anchors for your memories, each with its own story to tell.

- Keep a small pouch or envelope in your journal to collect ticket stubs, postcards, or other memorabilia.
- Use sketches or quick doodles to capture scenes or objects that catch your eye, adding a visual dimension to your narrative.
- Write down interesting bits of conversations or thoughts that cross your mind as you explore, offering a glimpse into your inner world during these moments.

Reflections on Movement

Travel, in its essence, is movement—not just through spaces but through states of mind and realms of emotion. Reflecting on how your journeys, whether to a distant city or just down the street, affect you offers profound insights into your personal growth and how you relate to the world. It's about recognizing the shifts within you as you move through different environments, meeting new faces, and encountering diverse ways of life.

- After each outing or trip, dedicate time to reflect on how the experience impacted you. Did it challenge your perceptions, evoke nostalgia, or inspire a new interest?
- Note the interactions with people you meet along the way. Often, it's these encounters that leave the most lasting impressions.

Planning Future Journeys

Your journal also serves as a canvas for dreaming up future adventures. It becomes a place to map out the places you wish to explore, weaving together aspirations and practicalities into a vision for future explorations. This proactive approach to travel journaling not only fuels your wanderlust but also helps crystallize vague desires into tangible plans.

- Create a bucket list of places you'd like to visit, both near and far, detailing why each destination calls to you.
- For each place on your list, jot down potential activities, sights to see, and local dishes to try, turning your journal into a preliminary itinerary that excites and inspires.

In every nook and cranny of our world lies a story waiting to be discovered, experienced, and chronicled. Travel journaling, in all its forms, is a celebration of these stories, an acknowledgment of the beauty and richness that surrounds us, if only we're willing to look. It reminds us that adventure doesn't demand grand expeditions.

Sometimes, it's just a matter of stepping out the door with open eyes and an open heart, ready to document the journey that unfolds.

2.9 Audio Journaling: An Alternative Approach

In a world that sings in the key of hustle, finding a moment to pause and pen down our thoughts can seem like a luxury few can afford. Enter audio journaling, a harmonious blend of modern technology and age-old introspection. This method involves using voice recordings to capture the essence of your thoughts, emotions, and daily experiences. It's like having a conversation with your future self, one where every nuance of emotion and every shade of meaning is preserved in the timbre of your voice.

Integrating Technology

The leap from pen and paper to voice memos might seem vast, but it's bridged by the sheer convenience and immediacy that audio journaling offers. With just a smartphone, you're equipped to document your life in real-time. This could mean recording a burst of inspiration during your morning walk, capturing the ambient sounds of a place that moves you, or simply recounting the day's events as you unwind. The key here is the seamless integration of journaling into your daily life, making it an accessible practice rather than a task that demands a set time and space.

- Utilize voice memo apps available on most smartphones or dedicated audio journaling apps that offer additional features like organization by date or theme.
- Experiment with different settings or times for your recordings; some might find a quiet evening at home ideal, while others might prefer recording amidst the hustle of their day to capture a more authentic vibe.

Benefits of Audio Recording

Audio journaling, with its ability to capture the human voice, offers a richness of expression that written words might not fully encompass. The laughter that bubbles up as you recount a humorous incident, the catch in your throat as you speak of something tender, or the excitement that colors your voice when you talk about a new discovery—these are the textures of life that audio journaling captures with fidelity. Moreover, the spontaneity of spoken thoughts often leads to a stream of consciousness, where insights surface naturally, unfiltered and uninhibited.

- The tone and emotion in your voice can add a layer of depth to your journal entries, making the process of revisiting them more immersive.
- Audio recordings capture your thoughts in real-time, often leading to a more spontaneous and candid reflection of your experiences.

Transcribing Highlights

While audio journaling stands on its own as a powerful tool for self-expression, marrying it with traditional journaling can create a comprehensive reflective practice. Transcribing key moments from your recordings not only allows you to engage with your thoughts on a deeper level but also makes certain insights or memories more accessible. This hybrid approach combines the immediacy and emotional depth of audio with the contemplative nature of writing.

- Regularly listen to your recordings and note down moments that strike you as particularly insightful or meaningful.
- Consider using transcription apps or services for longer recordings to streamline the process.

Privacy and Reflection

The intimate nature of audio journaling brings with it considerations of privacy and security. Unlike written journals that can be tucked away, digital recordings exist in a realm that feels inherently more exposed. However, many apps offer encryption, password protection, and other security measures to keep your personal reflections safe. Beyond privacy, the act of listening back to your own voice offers a unique form of reflection. It's a dialogue with your past self, one where the passage of time offers new perspectives on old thoughts.

- Choose audio journaling apps with strong security features to ensure your recordings remain private.
- Set aside time for playback sessions, approaching your past recordings with an open mind and heart, ready to glean new insights from old reflections.

In weaving audio journaling into the fabric of your life, you open a door to a form of self-expression that is both immediate and deeply personal. It's a testament to the power of voice as a medium for capturing the human experience, offering a dynamic and flexible way to document your journey through life. Whether used in tandem with traditional journaling or as a standalone practice, audio journaling enriches the narrative of your days, ensuring no emotion, thought, or moment is lost to time.

2.10 Photographic Journaling for the Visual Soul

In a world where every moment flashes by in an instant, capturing those fleeting snippets of life becomes a pursuit of the heart. Photographic journaling, a vivid tapestry woven with the threads of images, offers a pause button to the rapid pace of our days. It invites us to freeze time, if only for a second, and to hold onto the emotions, the landscapes, and the faces that color our existence.

Capturing Moments

Think of your camera, whether it be a high-tech DSLR, a simple point-and-shoot, or the smartphone in your pocket, as your brush, and the world around you as your canvas. The act of capturing a moment through photography is an intimate dance between the observer and the observed, a way to not just see but to truly notice the world. It's about finding beauty in the mundane, spotting a story unfolding on a crowded street, or seeing the play of shadows and light in your living room. Each snapshot is a piece of a larger puzzle, a frame in the movie of your life.

- Look for the extraordinary in the ordinary. A raindrop suspended on a leaf, or the smile of a stranger can be as captivating as a mountain vista.
- Embrace spontaneity. Some of the most profound moments are unplanned and unposed.

Storytelling Through Images

Photographs have the power to narrate without uttering a single word. They evoke emotions, set a scene, and tell a tale, all within the confines of their borders. This silent storytelling is a cornerstone of photographic journaling. A series of images can chronicle a day's adventure, capture the essence of a journey, or convey the depth of an emotion felt in a fleeting moment. The narrative woven through these visual elements is as rich and complex as any written story, inviting the observer to step into the frame and experience the moment as if they were there.

- Sequence your photos to create a narrative flow, leading the viewer through your story from beginning to end.
- Use captions sparingly, letting the images speak for themselves and only guiding the narrative when necessary.

Integrating Photos and Text

While photographs can stand alone as powerful storytellers, combining them with text elevates the journaling experience, creating a multimodal diary that engages both the visual and the literary senses. This blend offers a fuller, more nuanced exploration of your experiences, thoughts, and emotions. You might pair a photo with a haiku that it inspired, jot down the backstory of a candid snapshot, or reflect on the emotions a landscape evoked in you. This marriage of word and image opens up new dimensions of expression, making your journal a rich, layered testament to your life's journey.

- Pair each photo with a reflection, exploring why it resonates with you or what it represents about your current life chapter.
- Use photos as prompts for longer entries, letting the image guide your writing and uncover depths you might not have explored otherwise.

Reflecting on the Visual Journey

Flipping through the pages of your photographic journal offers a journey back in time, a visual chronicle of your growth, adventures, and the ever-changing tapestry of your life. It's a reflective practice that not only preserves memories but also offers insights into your evolution as a person. You might notice shifts in perspective, changes in what captures your attention, or developments in your photographic and narrative voice. This reflection is not just about reminiscing; it's about recognizing and appreciating the person you were at each moment and the person you are becoming.

- Set aside time regularly to review your journal, noting patterns, themes, and changes in your photographic and writing styles.
- Consider what your images and paired reflections reveal about your journey, using these insights to inform future paths and explorations.

In essence, photographic journaling is a celebration of life's richness, captured one frame at a time. It's a practice that encourages us to look closer, feel deeper, and connect more intimately with the world around us. Through the lens of our cameras, we not only preserve the moments that make up our days but also discover new layers of meaning and connection in our lives. As we move forward, let's carry with us the understanding that each snapshot, each word penned beside it, is a stitch in the vibrant quilt of our existence, a quilt we continue to weave with every click of the shutter and stroke of the pen.

As we close this chapter, let's remember: our lives are a mosaic of moments, each one precious, each one fleeting. Photographic journaling allows us to capture these moments, to hold them close and to reflect on the journey they represent. It's a practice that marries the visual with the verbal, creating a tapestry of memories and insights that are uniquely ours. As we turn the page, let's carry forward the spirit of observation, the joy of discovery, and the depth of reflection that photographic journaling nurtures within us.

Chapter 3

Making Journaling a Habit

So there I was, staring at my journal, the same one I vowed to write in every single day. It was collecting dust, a stark reminder of a promise not kept. Sounds familiar? We've all been there, fired up to start journaling regularly, only to watch our enthusiasm wane like the last slice of pizza at a party. But here's the thing: making journaling a habit isn't about monumental shifts or grand declarations. It's about setting up small, achievable goals and finding joy in the simplicity of marking pen on paper, day by day.

3.1 Setting Realistic Journaling Goals

The first step in weaving journaling into the fabric of your daily life is setting goals that don't set you up for a tumble. Think of your journaling habit like planting a garden. You wouldn't start by planting every type of seed you can find, right? You'd start small, maybe with some herbs on a windowsill, and nurture your way up from there.

Defining Achievable Targets

Setting a goal to journal for an hour every day might sound impressive, but is it realistic? Instead, aim for something more manageable. Five minutes before bed or three sentences about your day is a great start. Remember, the aim is consistency, not volume. Small daily entries can be just as impactful as longer, less frequent bursts of writing.

Flexibility in Frequency

Life happens. Some days are packed from dawn till dusk, while others stretch out with more room for reflection. Your journaling practice should flex with your schedule, not against it. Maybe you write daily during quieter weeks and scale back to a few times a week when life picks up. The key here is keeping the pen moving, even if it's just to jot down a single thought or feeling.

Celebrating Small Wins

Every time you make an entry, no matter how brief, give yourself a mental high-five. Completed three days of journaling in a row? Awesome. Managed to write something every day for a week? Even better. These milestones, as tiny as they may seem, are huge in building a lasting habit. Consider treating yourself to a small reward after reaching certain milestones—a new pen, a fancy coffee, or time to indulge in your favorite book.

Adjusting Goals as Needed

Your journaling goals should evolve with you. What works this month might not fit next month, and that's okay. Regularly take a moment to reflect on your journaling practice. Is it still serving you? Does it feel like a chore? Adjust your goals accordingly, always aiming for that sweet spot where journaling feels like a rewarding part of your day.

Visual Element: Goal-Setting Chart

To help you visualize and track your progress, I recommend creating a goal-setting chart in your journal. It could look something like this:

- **Week 1**: Aim to write at least three sentences daily.
- **Week 2**: Introduce one weekly reflection, looking back on the past seven days.
- **Week 3**: Try adding one doodle or sketch to your entries.
- **Reward**: After completing three weeks, treat yourself to a new journal or a set of pens.

This chart isn't just a tool; it's a visual reminder of your journey, marking each small step towards making journaling a seamless part of your routine.

Interactive Element: Journaling Prompts

To kickstart your journaling habit, here are a few prompts. Try to tackle one each day for a week:

1. What made you smile today?
2. Describe a moment today when you felt proud of yourself.
3. Write about a challenge you faced. How did it make you feel?
4. What's something you're looking forward to?
5. List three things you're grateful for today.
6. Describe your perfect day. What would you do, see, and feel?
7. Reflect on the past week. What were the highs and lows?

These prompts are your jumping-off points, simple nudges to get the ink flowing. Remember, there's no right or wrong way to answer them; what matters is the act of writing itself.

Making journaling a habit isn't about crafting perfect entries or filling up notebooks at breakneck speed. It's about finding a rhythm that works for you, one that brings a sense of fulfillment, reflection, and maybe a bit of fun into your daily grind. So, grab that journal, set some goals, and let's turn the everyday into something worth writing about.

3.2 The Five-Minute Morning Journal

Imagine the first light of dawn streaming through your window, a cup of something warm within arm's reach, and the quiet promise of a new day laying untouched before you. This is the moment the Five-Minute Morning Journal comes to life, a simple yet powerful practice designed to infuse your mornings with intention, reflection, and a dash of gratitude. It's about greeting the day not with a rush, but with a moment of stillness that sets a positive tone for all the hours to follow.

Cultivating a Morning Ritual

There's something almost sacred about the morning, a time when the world feels fresh and possibilities seem endless. Incorporating a brief journaling session into this time can transform it from just another part of your routine to a cherished ritual. Think of it as a daily check-in with yourself, a way to align your thoughts and intentions before the day's demands take hold. This practice doesn't ask for much—just five minutes, a pen, and your journal. In those quiet moments, you create a space to breathe, to dream, and to set the course for your day.

Prompt Suggestions

To ensure your Five-Minute Morning Journal is as effective as it is brief, having a set of go-to prompts can be incredibly helpful. These prompts are designed to spark reflection and set a positive mindset for the day ahead. Here are a few to get you started:

- **Today, I'm looking forward to...**: Identifying something, big or small, that you're excited about can infuse your day with a sense of anticipation and joy.
- **One word to describe how I want to feel today is...**: This helps you focus on the emotional tone you wish to set for your day.
- **Today, I will let go of...**: Letting go of a worry or a negative thought can make room for more positive experiences.
- **My intention for today is...**: Setting a clear intention acts as a guidepost for your actions and decisions throughout the day.

Benefits of Morning Journaling

Kicking off your day with a journaling session, even one as brief as five minutes, comes with a host of benefits. For starters, it boosts mindfulness, encouraging you to live in the present and engage more deeply with your surroundings. It also enhances productivity by helping you prioritize your tasks and focus on what truly matters. On a deeper level, this morning ritual fosters a sense of self-awareness, allowing you to connect with your thoughts and feelings before the external noise of the day sets in. Perhaps most importantly, it cultivates a mindset of positivity and gratitude, acting as a gentle reminder that every day is a gift filled with potential.

Incorporating Gratitude

Gratitude is the golden thread that can weave joy into the fabric of our daily lives, and the morning journal is the perfect place to start this practice. Each morning, dedicate a part of your journaling to noting down at least one thing you're grateful for. It could be as simple as the warmth of your bed or the taste of your morning coffee. This act of recognizing and appreciating the everyday blessings in your life can dramatically shift your perspective, opening your eyes to the abundance that surrounds you. Over time, this practice not only makes you more attuned to the positive aspects of your day but also contributes to an overall sense of well-being and contentment.

In the soft glow of morning, your Five-Minute Morning Journal becomes a beacon of intention, reflection, and gratitude. It's a practice that doesn't demand much of your time but offers back immensely in terms of clarity, focus, and a deep-seated appreciation for the life you lead. As the days unfold, this simple ritual has the power to transform not just your mornings, but your entire approach to life, one sunrise at a time.

3.3 Night Reflections: Ending Your Day on Paper

When the sun dips below the horizon and the world quiets, there's a special kind of magic that stirs in the act of recounting the day's events on paper. This isn't about cataloging every minute detail but rather capturing the essence of your day, the moments that moved you, challenged you, or brought you joy. It's in these quiet evening hours that your journal becomes more than a collection of pages; it becomes a vessel for introspection and growth.

The Power of Evening Reflection

There's something inherently therapeutic about pouring your thoughts onto paper as the day winds down. It's a process that allows you to offload not just the events that unfolded but the emotions and thoughts that accompanied them. This act of evening reflection serves as a mental decompression, a way to sift through the clutter of the day and make sense of your experiences. It's about acknowledging your feelings, celebrating your achievements, and learning from the challenges you faced.

In this sacred space between day and night, your journal stands as a beacon, guiding you through your thoughts and offering clarity. It's a practice that not only aids in unwinding but also enriches your understanding of yourself and the world around you.

Structured Reflection Prompts

To deepen your evening reflection, consider incorporating structured prompts into your practice. These prompts are designed to peel back the layers of your day, revealing insights and lessons hidden beneath the surface. Here are a few to get you started:

- **Today I felt...**: Explore the range of emotions you experienced, from the highs to the lows.
- **A challenge I faced was...**: Reflect on any obstacles you encountered and how they made you feel or react.
- **Something I learned today...**: Identify any new insights or knowledge gained, no matter how big or small.
- **I'm proud of myself for...**: Celebrate your victories and moments of strength or kindness.

These prompts are steppingstones, guiding you through a reflective journey that illuminates the day's events and your responses to them.

Preparing for Rest

As you spill ink across the pages of your journal, recounting the day's tales, you're also setting the stage for a peaceful night's rest. This practice of evening journaling can be a powerful ally in your sleep hygiene, creating a mental separation between the day's activities and the quiet of night. It's a ritual that signals to your brain that it's time to slow down, to let go of the day's worries and prepare for rest.

In this transition, your journal acts not just as a repository for your thoughts but as a tool for mindfulness, drawing your focus inward and away from the external noise. It's a gentle reminder that no matter how tumultuous your day was, the page offers a fresh start, a blank slate awaiting tomorrow's stories.

Learning from the Day

Perhaps the most profound aspect of ending your day on paper is the opportunity it presents for learning and personal growth. Each entry, each sentence penned, is a mirror reflecting back at you the lessons of the day. It's in these reflections that you find the seeds of growth, understanding not just the events that unfolded but how they shaped you.

- **Analyzing reactions and decisions**: Through your reflections, you gain insight into how you react to different situations and why, offering a chance to consider alternative approaches or affirm positive ones.
- **Identifying patterns**: Over time, your evening entries can reveal patterns in your thoughts, behaviors, and emotions, shedding light on aspects of your life that may need attention or change.
- **Fostering gratitude**: Amidst the recounting of challenges and lessons, there's also space to recognize and appreciate the good, fostering a habit of gratitude that enriches your life.

By turning introspection into a nightly ritual, you not only document your journey but actively engage in shaping it. You learn from the past, find peace in the present, and lay the groundwork for the future.

In the quietude that bookends your day, your journal holds space for all that you've experienced, felt, and learned. It's in these pages that you find a sense of closure for the day that's passed and a readiness to greet the new day ahead. Through the simple act of reflecting, you weave together the threads of your life, creating a tapestry rich with insight, growth, and understanding.

3.4 The Lunch Break Quick Journal

Picture this: you're halfway through a whirlwind of a day, the morning's caffeine buzz has worn off, and your to-do list seems to be looking at you with a smirk, knowing well it's far from conquered. Here lies the perfect moment, nestled between the hustle of morning tasks and the afternoon's sprint, for what I like to call the Lunch Break Quick Journal. It's your secret weapon against the chaos, a brief respite that not only rejuvenates but also aligns your thoughts, ensuring you tackle the rest of the day with renewed vigor and clarity.

Utilizing Breaks Productively

Let's face it, the middle of the day often finds us at a crossroads of energy levels; too far from the morning's start to feel fresh, yet too early to see the finish line. Seizing this moment for a quick journal session can transform it from a slump into a springboard. It doesn't demand much – just a few minutes to pause, breathe, and reflect.

This pause acts as a reset button, giving you not only a well-deserved break but also an opportunity to recalibrate your focus for the afternoon ahead.

Prompt Ideas for Short Sessions

To maximize the benefits of these brief interludes, having a set of go-to prompts can steer your thoughts and keep your sessions engaging. Here are a few to spark your midday muse:

- **One thing I've accomplished today that I'm proud of is...**: Recognizing your morning achievements fuels motivation.
- **A situation I handled well/not so well this morning was...**: Reflection fosters learning and adjustment.
- **An unexpected challenge I encountered today was...**: Helps in mentally preparing for similar future surprises.
- **Something I'm looking forward to after work is...**: Keeps you connected to life beyond the office.
- **One way I can make the rest of my day better is...**: Encourages proactive thinking and positivity.

These prompts are quick divers, plunging straight into the heart of your day's narrative and resurfacing with pearls of wisdom that might otherwise remain unseen beneath the waves of busyness.

Portable Journaling Kits

The logistics of lunch break journaling hinge on one crucial element: portability. A streamlined journaling kit can make all the difference, turning a good intention into a seamless habit. Here's what you might include:

- **A compact journal**: Size matters; think pocket-sized or a small notebook that easily slips into your bag.
- **A multi-use pen**: Why carry three pens when one can do the job? Look for those that feature a ballpoint, highlighter, and stylus.
- **Sticky notes**: Perfect for jotting down thoughts that you might want to transfer or expand on later.
- **A small pouch**: Keeps your journaling kit together and can double as a handy storage for your headphones – a perfect companion for those who like to journal to music.

This kit becomes your mobile command center, ready at a moment's notice to anchor you back to a state of mindfulness and creativity, no matter where you are.

Mindfulness in the Midst of Chaos

Now, to the heart of the matter: why integrate journaling into this specific slice of your day? The answer lies in the power of midday mindfulness. Just as a storm finds its eye, the day's center can be a point of calm, offering a unique opportunity to ground your thoughts and emotions. This practice, brief as it may be, is a testament to the transformative power of pausing. It's a reminder that amidst deadlines and demands, there exists a space for you to realign with your intentions, to shift gears from reactive to proactive, and to approach the rest of your day not as a series of tasks but as a canvas awaiting your mark.

In these moments of reflection, you'll find not just a break from the noise but a bridge. A bridge that connects the morning's efforts with the afternoon's potential, ensuring that as the day unfolds, it does so not just with your participation but with your direction. This shift, subtle yet significant, can redefine not just your day but your relationship with time itself, teaching you that within every day lies a moment waiting to be claimed, a moment that holds the key to balance, focus, and perhaps most importantly, to peace.

As your day marches on, let this practice of lunch break journaling be your haven, a space where time slows, even if just for a breath, allowing you to gather yourself before diving back into the fray. Here, in the simple act of pen meeting paper, you'll find a wellspring of clarity and calm, proving that sometimes, the mightiest tools come in the quietest moments.

3.5 Using Journaling Prompts Effectively

In the woven tapestry of our lives, each thread represents a story, an emotion, a fleeting thought waiting to be captured. Yet, there are days when the loom sits idle, our minds grappling with the silence of a blank page. Here, journaling prompts act as the shuttle, weaving through the warp and weft of our consciousness, teasing out stories and insights hidden in the fabric of our daily lives. They're not just questions or statements; they're keys unlocking the doors to self-discovery, reflection, and creativity.

The Role of Prompts

On those days when inspiration seems as distant as a forgotten melody, prompts serve as a gentle nudge, steering our thoughts and guiding our pens across the page. They're particularly potent when the well of creativity feels dry, offering a starting point that can lead to unexpected journeys. Think of them as seeds; from one small prompt, a whole garden of thoughts can bloom, each branch and leaf a new direction for your writing to take.

Creating a Prompt Bank

Imagine having a treasure chest, its contents glimmering with potential. This is your prompt bank, a collection of ideas, questions, and challenges ready to spark your creativity at a moment's notice. Building this cache is both an exercise in foresight and a gift to your future self. Start by jotting down prompts as they come to you, whether from books, conversations, or moments of reflection. Online communities and journaling apps are wellsprings of inspiration, offering an abundance of prompts tailored to every interest and mood.

Organize your prompts by theme—emotions, memories, dreams, daily life—and revisit them often, adding new finds and discarding those that no longer resonate. Your prompt bank is a living entity, evolving as you do, always ready to offer the right key for the lock that is your current state of mind.

Sharing Prompts with a Community

The act of journaling, often solitary, blooms in unexpected ways when shared within a community. Prompts become sparks flying from one mind to another, igniting creativity and connection. Sharing prompts with fellow journalers can transform them, imbuing them with new meanings and perspectives shaped by the collective experience.

Consider starting a journaling circle, either in person or online, where members exchange prompts and reflections. Social media platforms and journaling forums offer spaces for such exchanges, creating a tapestry of inspiration woven from the diverse threads of individual experiences. This communal aspect adds depth to your practice, reminding you that while the journey of self-discovery may be personal, you're not traversing it alone.

Prompt Adaptation

The true magic of a prompt lies in its adaptability, its ability to be molded and reshaped to fit the contours of your current life narrative. A prompt that asks, "What are you grateful for today?" can morph into a reflection on gratitude's role in resilience, or an exploration of the small joys that stitch our days together. Adapting prompts encourages you to view them not as rigid directives but as open-ended questions, each with a multitude of answers as unique as the person penning them down.

When encountering a prompt, ask yourself:

- How does this resonate with what I'm feeling or experiencing right now?
- What new perspective or angle can I explore in response to this prompt?
- Is there a memory, dream, or future aspiration that this prompt brings to the surface?

By treating prompts as flexible guides rather than fixed points, you invite a richness and diversity into your journaling that mirrors the complexity of human experience. It's in this flexibility that prompts reveal their true power, acting as companions and catalysts on your journey of self-expression and exploration.

In the dance of pen on paper, prompts are the rhythm, guiding our words and thoughts in a symphony of introspection and creativity. They remind us that every blank page is an opportunity, every unformed thought a potential masterpiece waiting to be uncovered. As we continue to weave the tapestry of our lives, let these prompts be the shuttle in our hands, turning the ordinary into the extraordinary, one word at a time.

3.6 Creating a Dedicated Journaling Space

Have you ever tried to write in the middle of chaos, with noise buzzing around like a persistent fly you just can't swat away? Or maybe you've attempted to pen down your deepest thoughts with family members popping in every five minutes, asking if you've seen the remote. Not exactly conducive to a flood of inspiration, is it? That's precisely why carving out a dedicated space for journaling, a little sanctuary where your thoughts can flow uninterrupted, is less of a luxury and more of a necessity.

Importance of a Sacred Space

Think of your journaling spot as sacred ground. This is where the magic happens, where words paint the blank canvas of your journal, transforming it into a tapestry of thoughts, dreams, and reflections. A designated space signals to your brain that it's time to shift gears, moving from the hustle-bustle of daily life into a more introspective mode. It's about creating an environment where your mind feels at ease, free to explore the corridors of your imagination without the fear of intrusion or distraction.

Personalizing Your Space

Now, creating this nook doesn't mean you need a lavish study overlooking the ocean (though wouldn't that be nice?). It's about making the space distinctly yours. Start with comfort – a cozy chair, a cushion that just feels right, or even a spot on the floor with a plush rug. Next, add elements that spark joy or inspiration. It could be:

- **Photos** that remind you of happy times or people you love.
- **Plants** to bring a bit of nature indoors, adding a sense of calm and freshness.
- **Inspirational quotes** artfully displayed to give you that little nudge when you're grasping for words.
- **Soft lighting**, perhaps a lamp that casts just enough glow to write by without straining your eyes, creating an ambiance that invites creativity.

Portable Spaces

Not everyone has the luxury of dedicating a permanent spot in their home for journaling, and that's perfectly okay. The beauty of journaling is its adaptability. For those with space constraints or who find themselves constantly on the move, consider a portable journaling kit. This could include a small bag or box containing your journal, favorite pens, a compact folding seat pad, and even a portable lamp. With your kit in hand, the world becomes your journaling oasis. A bench in the park, a quiet corner in a café, or even your car parked in a scenic spot can serve as the perfect backdrop for your writing escapades.

The Role of Atmosphere

Never underestimate the power of atmosphere. It's not just about the physical space but also about the ambiance. The right atmosphere can whisk you away from the mundane, wrapping you in a cocoon of creativity. Consider these elements:

- **Lighting**: Soft, warm light can make a space feel inviting, while natural light boosts mood and energy. Experiment to find what works best for you.
- **Sounds**: Some prefer the absolute quiet, while others flourish with background noise. Whether it's the gentle hum of a coffee shop, the soothing sounds of nature, or a carefully curated playlist, the right sound landscape can significantly enhance your journaling experience.
- **Scents**: Aromatherapy can play a surprising role in setting the mood for journaling. The scent of lavender can calm, peppermint can invigorate, and the smell of old books... well, that's just a delight for the senses.

By thoughtfully crafting your journaling space, you're not just setting up a place to write. You're building a retreat, a personal haven where the outside world gently fades away, leaving you in the company of your thoughts and musings. It's about creating a spot where you feel utterly at ease, where inspiration flows freely, and where your journal eagerly awaits the stories only you can tell.

3.7 Journaling with a Partner or Friend

Imagine transforming your solitary journaling practice into a shared voyage of discovery and connection. This is where the concept of journaling with a partner or friend comes into play, an idea that might seem unconventional at first glance but one that holds the potential to deepen relationships and foster mutual growth. It's about opening up new channels of communication, offering insights into each other's thoughts, dreams, and struggles, all through the intimate medium of journaling.

Shared Journaling Experience

The beauty of sharing your journaling journey with someone else lies in the unique blend of intimacy and creativity it brings to a relationship. Whether it's a friend, a family member, or a partner, journaling together creates a space for vulnerability and understanding. It can be as simple as exchanging journals to read each other's entries, or as collaborative as working on a joint journal, where both contribute thoughts, reflections, and artwork. This shared space becomes a testament to your journey together, a place where individual growth and collective bond intertwine.

Guidelines for Respectful Sharing

Navigating the shared territory of a journal requires a foundation of trust and respect. Here are some ground rules to ensure a positive and respectful sharing experience:

- **Consent is key**: Always ask for permission before reading each other's entries, and respect any boundaries set.
- **Privacy matters**: Agree on what parts of the journal are open for sharing and what stays private. It's okay to have areas that are off-limits.
- **Non-judgemental stance**: Approach each other's entries with an open mind and heart, avoiding criticism or unsolicited advice.
- **Confidentiality is crucial**: What's shared in the journal stays between the two of you, safeguarding the sanctity of your shared stories.

Collaborative Journaling Activities

To make the most out of your shared journaling, try incorporating activities and prompts that foster connection and mutual understanding. Here are a few ideas:

- **Write a letter to each other**: Pen down your thoughts, appreciation, or hopes for the other person and share them in your journal.
- **Document a shared experience**: Whether it's a trip, a movie night, or a cooking adventure, write about the experience from each of your perspectives.
- **Create a 'question of the week' tradition**: Take turns asking a question that both of you answer, ranging from light-hearted to deep and introspective.
- **Artistic collaboration**: Dedicate a page where one starts a drawing or painting, and the other completes it, blending your creative energies.

Reflecting on the Shared Journey

As you navigate this path of shared journaling, it's essential to periodically reflect on how this practice is shaping your relationship and personal growth. Consider discussing questions like:

- How has journaling together brought us closer?
- What have we learned about each other that we didn't know before?
- In what ways has this experience influenced our individual journaling practices?
- How can we further enrich our shared journaling journey?

These reflections not only reinforce the value of journaling as a tool for relationship building but also ensure that both individuals feel heard, appreciated, and connected.

In essence, journaling with a partner or friend opens up a world where words and emotions flow freely, creating bridges of understanding and empathy. It's a practice that celebrates the individual narratives within the context of a shared journey, enriching the tapestry of your relationship with every word penned and every page turned. Together, you embark on an adventure that not only captures the moments and memories you share but also fosters an environment of mutual support and growth.

3.8 Keeping a Journal at Work

In the bustling corridors of our professional lives, where deadlines loom and meetings cascade one after the other, lies a secret weapon that might just tilt the scales in favor of clarity, productivity, and peace. This secret weapon? A work journal. Far from the personal diaries we confide in after hours, a work journal serves as a compass through the complexities of our careers, guiding us through reflections, goals, and the myriad challenges we face.

Journaling for Professional Growth

Imagine your work journal as a garden where the seeds of professional aspirations are sown. Each entry, a meticulous record of your ambitions, triumphs, and lessons learned, blossoms into a roadmap guiding your career's trajectory. But this garden thrives on more than just recounting successes; it's fertilized by the reflections on setbacks, the strategies devised to overcome them, and the clarity gained in the process.

- **Goal Mapping**: Dedicate pages to outlining your short-term and long-term career goals. Break these down into actionable steps, revisiting and refining them as you progress.
- **Achievement Log**: Make it a habit to record your accomplishments, no matter how small they may seem. This log serves as a powerful reminder of your capabilities, especially on days filled with doubt.
- **Skill Development**: Use your journal to track your learning journey. Note down new skills you've acquired, courses attended, or areas for improvement. This continuous record not only highlights your growth but also pinpoints areas ripe for development.

Mindfulness in the Workplace

In the whirlwind of workday pressures, a journal can be your anchor, grounding you in mindfulness and serenity. By carving out moments to jot down thoughts, reflect on interactions, or simply breathe and be present, you're integrating a practice of mindfulness into your professional life. This habit not only reduces stress but also enhances focus, allowing you to approach tasks with a clear mind and a centered spirit.

- **Daily Reflections**: Before diving into your to-do list, take a few minutes to jot down what you're feeling. Are you anxious about a presentation? Excited about a new project? Acknowledging these emotions can help manage them more effectively.
- **Gratitude Entries**: Amidst the hustle, it's easy to overlook the positives. Regularly noting aspects of your job you're thankful for can shift your perspective, fostering a more fulfilling work experience.

Navigating Professional Challenges

Every career path is dotted with hurdles. Yet, within your work journal lies a space to dissect these challenges, to strategize solutions and glean insights from each obstacle faced. This reflective practice not only aids in problem-solving but also in personal and professional growth, turning stumbling blocks into steppingstones.

- **Challenge Analysis**: When confronted with a hurdle, detail it in your journal. What is the issue? Why is it impacting you? How have you attempted to address it? This analysis can unearth underlying patterns or solutions previously overlooked.
- **Success Strategies**: After overcoming a challenge, document the strategy that led to your success. This becomes a personal playbook of sorts, a repository of tactics that worked, ready to be deployed when future challenges arise.

Maintaining Privacy

While a work journal is a treasure trove of insights and reflections, it also contains sensitive information that necessitates discretion. Ensuring the confidentiality of your entries is paramount to maintaining trust and privacy in the workplace.

- **Physical Security**: Opt for journals with locks or store them in a secure location, away from prying eyes. If you prefer digital journaling, ensure files are password protected or encrypted.
- **Discretion in Entries**: Be mindful of how you phrase reflections, especially those involving colleagues or workplace dynamics. Focus on personal growth and strategies rather than venting frustrations that could be misconstrued if read by others.

In the tapestry of our professional lives, a work journal emerges as a vital thread, weaving together our aspirations, challenges, and victories. It's a space where growth is plotted, resilience is built, and mindfulness is cultivated amidst the cacophony of daily tasks. By integrating this practice into your work routine, you're not just navigating your career with more clarity and focus; you're also crafting a legacy of professional development, one entry at a time.

3.9 On-the-Go Journaling Solutions

In a world that doesn't pause, finding a moment to breathe, let alone journal, seems like a quest for the impossible. Yet, the beauty of journaling lies in its fluidity, its ability to mold itself around the contours of our bustling lives. Here, we explore the art of journaling anytime, anywhere, ensuring that even in the whirlwind of daily commitments, our thoughts find a harbor.

Journaling Anytime, Anywhere

The secret to weaving journaling into the fabric of a packed schedule is recognizing the pockets of unused time scattered throughout the day. That ten-minute coffee break, the waiting room before an appointment, the quiet minutes before sleep claims you—each holds the potential for reflection. The trick is to shift our perception, seeing these not as gaps to be filled with scrolling through our phones but as opportunities to connect with ourselves. This mindset transforms journaling from an additional task to a seamlessly integrated part of daily life, a moment of calm in the storm.

Digital Journaling Apps

For the modern-day journaler, digital platforms offer a bridge over the river of excuses—"I don't have my journal with me," "I'm too busy to write." Enter digital journaling apps, the convenient, portable solution to journaling on the go. These apps are designed with the mobile user in mind, offering features like:

- **Sync across devices**: Start an entry on your phone during your commute and finish it on your laptop at home.
- **Password protection**: Keep your thoughts safe from prying eyes.
- **Customizable templates**: Whether you're capturing a day's events or logging gratitude, there's a template for that.
- **Prompt generators**: Stuck for what to write? Let the app nudge your inspiration.

When choosing an app, consider what features matter most to you. Is it the ease of organizing entries by date or topic? Perhaps it's the ability to add photos or voice notes. The right app turns your phone into a digital journal, always at hand, ready when you are.

Voice-to-Text Options

In the symphony of life, our hands are often tied—literally. Driving, cooking, or cradling a baby, these moments don't lend themselves to traditional journaling. This is where voice-to-text technology shines, allowing us to capture thoughts without lifting a pen. Modern smartphones and digital journaling apps come equipped with voice recognition, transforming spoken words into written entries. It's a liberating feeling, speaking your thoughts aloud, knowing they're being captured, ready to be reflected upon later. Perfect for the multitasker, this method ensures that journaling fits into your life, not the other way around.

Compact and Portable Journaling Kits

For purists who relish the feel of pen on paper, creating a portable journaling kit is akin to packing an emergency kit—essential and reassuring. A well-thought-out kit includes:

- **A small, lightweight journal**: Easy to carry, yet sturdy enough to withstand the journey.
- **A reliable pen**: Choose one that doesn't leak or run out quickly. Consider a pen with an attached clip for secure storage.
- **Sticky notes**: For those fleeting thoughts that you want to revisit or expand upon later.
- **A mini pouch**: To keep everything together. Opt for one with zip closure to avoid losing your pen or notes.

This kit becomes your loyal companion, sliding into your bag or backpack, ensuring that no matter where life takes you, your journal is just a zip away. Whether it's jotting down observations on a park bench or capturing a moment of inspiration on a train, your journaling practice remains uninterrupted, as vibrant and dynamic as life itself.

In crafting a journaling practice that moves with you, you're embracing the essence of adaptability, ensuring that your reflections and insights are captured in real-time, amidst the ebb and flow of daily life. This approach not only enriches your journaling experience but also embeds it more deeply into your routine, making reflection a natural part of your day, not an island in the stream.

3.10 Tracking Progress and Reflecting on Growth

In the dance of daily life, where routines spin us around and days blend into a blur, it's easy to lose sight of how far we've come, the obstacles we've hurdled, and the mountains we've climbed. It's here, in the quiet moments with our journal open before us, that we can pause and look back, tracing our steps, acknowledging our growth, and setting our sights on new horizons. This isn't just about reminiscing; it's about recognizing and understanding the journey we're on, celebrating our victories, and learning from the paths we've trodden.

The Importance of Reviewing Journals

Flipping through past journal entries is akin to opening a time capsule, each page a snapshot of who we were at that moment. It's a practice that unveils patterns in our thoughts and behaviors, illuminates how we've navigated challenges, and showcases the milestones we've reached. More than that, it reveals our resilience, our capacity for growth, and the subtle ways we evolve over time. Regularly revisiting these pages invites a deeper connection with ourselves, fostering an appreciation for our journey and the lessons learned along the way.

Creating a Reflection Ritual

Establishing a ritual for reflection transforms this practice from a sporadic activity into a meaningful cornerstone of our journaling journey. Setting aside a specific time, perhaps at the end of each month or season, creates a rhythm to this process, a dedicated moment to engage with our past selves and glean insights. During these sessions, consider pondering questions like:

- How have I grown since this entry?
- What challenges did I overcome, and how?
- What moments of joy and gratitude stand out?
- How have my goals and aspirations shifted?

These questions serve as guideposts, leading us through our reflections with intention and purpose, helping to distill the essence of our experiences and the growth they've spurred.

Celebrating Personal Milestones

Our journaling journey is dotted with milestones – some monumental, others seemingly minor, yet each significant in its own right. Acknowledging these achievements is crucial, for it reinforces the value of our efforts and the progress we've made. Celebrating these moments can take various forms, from dedicating a special entry to a particular achievement to sharing our milestones with loved ones. It's a practice that not only bolsters our sense of accomplishment but also imbues our journaling with a sense of purpose and joy.

Setting Future Intentions

With the insights gleaned from our reflections, we stand at the threshold of the future, ready to chart our course with intention and clarity. Our journal, a faithful companion on this journey, becomes the canvas upon which we sketch our aspirations. Drawing from our past experiences and the growth we've witnessed, we can set intentions that are not only aligned with who we are but also who we wish to become. This cyclical process of reflection, learning, and forward-looking sets a foundation for continuous growth and self-discovery, ensuring our journaling practice remains vibrant, purposeful, and deeply rewarding.

As we close this segment of our journey together, let's carry with us the understanding that journaling is more than a repository for our thoughts and experiences. It's a mirror reflecting our growth, a map guiding our way forward, and a testament to the resilience and strength within each of us. Through the simple act of putting pen to paper, we engage in a dialogue with ourselves that spans the past, present, and future, weaving a narrative that is uniquely ours. Let's step forward with confidence, knowing that each word we write is a step toward understanding, growth, and the endless possibilities that await.

Chapter 4

Painting Your Pages with Color

Ever had one of those moments where you're staring down a blank journal page, and it's staring back, almost challenging you? It's like being at a standoff with a spaghetti squash at dinner time—you know there's potential there but cracking it open to get to the good stuff feels daunting. The trick, as with the squash, lies in finding the right tool. In this case, it's not a kitchen utensil but something far more vibrant: color. Let's explore how color not only breaks the ice with your journal but also deepens the conversation you have with it.

4.1 Emotional Palette

Colors are more than just a feast for the eyes; they're a language of their own, whispering secrets about our inner landscapes. Ever noticed how a gray, drizzly day might tug on your mood strings, painting everything in a melancholic hue? Or how a clear, azure sky can lift your spirits? That's color at work, stirring emotions and memories within us. Diving into this colorful dialogue can transform your journaling experience, adding layers of depth and emotion to your entries. So, next time you pick up your journal, consider what color speaks to you in the moment and what it evokes. Is it the fiery passion of red, the serene wisdom of blue, or perhaps the sunny optimism of yellow?

Color of the Day

For a fun twist, try the "Color of the Day" exercise. Each morning, pick a color that resonates with how you feel or what you hope for the day. Use this color as your guide, integrating it into your journaling, whether through ink, paper, or art. As the day unfolds, pay attention to how this color appears in your life and the feelings it brings. Maybe you chose green and found yourself feeling more connected to nature during a walk, or perhaps pink had you noticing the warmth in your interactions. At day's end, reflect on these moments, letting the color stitch together the story of your day.

Mixing Mediums

Why stick to one tool when a whole toolbox awaits? Mixing mediums invites an exploration of textures, shades, and expressions, turning your journal into a playground of creativity. Here's how:

- Start with watercolor washes to set a soft, dreamy background. Watercolors blend and bleed in unpredictable ways, mirroring the fluidity of our thoughts.
- Add depth with colored pencils, sketching symbols or scenes that capture your day's essence. The precision of pencils allows for detailed storytelling.
- Highlight key moments or feelings with markers, their bold lines and vivid colors drawing attention to what matters most to you.

This mix not only enriches your journal's visual appeal but also enhances the storytelling, each medium bringing a different voice to the narrative.

Color-Themed Pages

Dedicating entire pages to a single-color theme can be both a challenge and a delight. It's an immersion, a deep dive into what a color means to you, how it feels, and the memories it conjures. Here's a way to approach it:

- Choose your color and gather materials in various shades and mediums.
- Reflect on what this color symbolizes in your life. Is it the calming blue of a cherished lake or the vibrant orange of autumn leaves crunching underfoot?
- Fill your page with these reflections, using only your chosen color. Incorporate images, textures, and words that embody the color's essence.

This exercise isn't just about creating a visually cohesive page; it's an exploration of the emotional and experiential spectrum that colors represent in our lives.

In the dance of journaling, color is more than just an embellishment. It's a partner, leading us through the rhythms of our emotions, memories, and dreams. It invites us to see beyond the black and white, to explore the rich tapestry of our lives in full spectrum. So next time you face off with that daunting blank page, remember, color is your ally, ready to unlock the stories waiting to be told.

4.2 Nature Sketching for the Non-Artist

Imagine you're out in the wild—or maybe just your backyard—and you spot a scene that tugs at your soul. There's an urge to capture it, not just in memory, but on paper. But then, the thought pops up, "I can't draw." Let's toss that thought aside and dive into how anyone, yes, even you, can sketch nature with a few simple tricks and a dash of patience.

Simplified Shapes

Every masterpiece begins with a simple line, a circle, or a squiggle. Nature, in all its intricate glory, can be broken down into these basic components. A tree isn't just a tree but a compilation of circles, lines, and ovals coming together in harmony. Begin by softly observing your chosen scene, squint a little if it helps, and start identifying these basic shapes within it. Your first sketch might look more like a child's drawing than a nature masterpiece, and that's perfectly fine. With each shape, you're laying the groundwork for your artistic confidence to bloom.

- Start with broad shapes, avoiding getting caught up in details.
- Think of your drawing as a puzzle, placing each simple shape to fit the scene.

Observation Over Perfection

The true essence of nature sketching isn't found in the accuracy of the strokes but in the act of observing itself. It's about the connection you forge with the scene before you, the way the leaves rustle in the wind, or how the shadows play on the ground. Let go of the notion that your sketch must be a faithful reproduction of the scene. Instead, focus on capturing the feel of the moment. This shift in perspective—from perfection to observation—opens up a world where every scribble tells a story and every blot of ink holds a memory.

- Prioritize capturing the essence over getting every detail right.
- Remind yourself that the goal is to connect with nature, not to create a perfect piece of art.

Adding Textures and Layers

Once you have your basic shapes down, it's time to bring your sketch to life with textures and layers. This is where your drawing begins to develop depth and character. Techniques like hatching (close parallel lines) and stippling (dots) are your friends here. They're surprisingly simple yet effective ways to add dimension to your sketches. Experiment with these techniques to create variations in shading and texture, giving your sketch a more dynamic look. For example, use tighter hatching for darker areas and lighter, spaced-out dots for lighter regions.

- Practice different textures on a separate paper to get a feel for what each technique can achieve.
- Apply these textures to your sketches sparingly at first, gradually building up layers to avoid overwhelming the drawing.

Incorporating Nature Finds

Here's where the magic happens. Integrating real elements from nature—like leaves, pressed flowers, or even a smudge of soil—into your journal pages can transform your sketches from mere drawings to multi-dimensional art pieces. This tactile aspect not only adds a unique flair to your work but also deepens the bond between your journaling practice and the natural world. Imagine a page adorned with a leaf rubbing, its intricate veins pressed into the paper, alongside a sketch of the tree it came from. It's a beautiful way to blend art with tangible pieces of the world around you.

- Experiment with placing leaves under your page and gently shading over them to capture their texture.
- Use a clear adhesive to secure delicate finds like pressed flowers, ensuring they become a lasting part of your journal.

Through these approaches, nature sketching evolves from a daunting task to an enjoyable exploration of the world around you. It's not about the final outcome but the joy found in the process, the calm that comes from connecting with nature, and the personal growth stemming from expressing your unique perspective. So, grab your journal, step outside, and let the beauty of the natural world unfold beneath your pen.

4.3 Writing Poetry in Your Journal

Imagine your journal as a canvas, not just for sketches or diary entries, but for the dance of poetry. Poetry, in its essence, is the distillation of emotion and experience into a few potent lines, a way to capture the fleeting moments and vast landscapes of the heart. Here, we're not just stringing words together; we're weaving magic, creating something that resonates on a deeply personal level. Let's explore how poetry can become a vibrant thread in the tapestry of your journaling practice.

Poetry as Expression

Poetry stands as a beacon for those navigating the tumultuous seas of emotion and experience. It's the art of distilling the complex, often messy human experience into lines that sing, that resonate, that stay with you long after the page is turned. Whether it's the sharp sting of loss, the soft warmth of love, or the quiet contemplation of a solitary moment, poetry offers a form that's as flexible as it is powerful. Your journal becomes not just a repository of thoughts but a garden where your poetic expressions bloom, each poem a snapshot of your inner world.

- Begin by identifying a moment or emotion you'd like to explore.
- Let yourself feel it fully, then reach for the words that come closest to capturing that sensation.

Free Verse Freedom

For those wary of strict rhymes or meter, free verse stands with open arms, inviting you to express yourself without the constraints of traditional poetic forms. Free verse is the wildflower meadow of poetry — it doesn't ask for neat rows or uniform blooms. Instead, it thrives on the raw, the uneven, the utterly personal. This freedom lets your thoughts flow unimpeded, allowing the natural rhythm of your voice to emerge.

- Start with a thought or image, then simply let the words flow.
- Don't worry about line lengths, rhymes, or structure. Let the content shape the form.

Found Poetry

There's poetry hidden in the everyday — in the pages of a dusty old book, in the conversations overheard at a café, even in the mundane texts of an instruction manual. Found poetry is the art of excavating these hidden gems, combining words and phrases from existing texts to create something new, something uniquely yours. It's a reminder that beauty and depth can be found in the most unexpected places.

- Gather texts from various sources — books, newspapers, magazines, even junk mail.
- Look for phrases that catch your eye or resonate with you emotionally.
- Combine these snippets into a poem, rearranging and playing with the order until it feels just right.

Haiku for Mindfulness

In the realm of poetic forms, the haiku stands out for its simplicity and depth. Originating from Japan, this form captures the essence of a moment, often with a focus on nature, in just three lines. The traditional structure — five syllables in the first line, seven in the second, and five in the third — encourages precision and mindfulness, urging you to observe the world around you with fresh eyes.

- Choose a moment or observation from nature or daily life.
- Convey the scene or emotion in just three lines, adhering to the 5-7-5 syllable structure.
- Embrace the challenge of saying more with less, letting the constraints heighten your creativity.

By inviting poetry into your journal, you're not just recording life; you're transforming it, finding the extraordinary in the ordinary, and giving voice to the silent choruses within. Whether through the free-flowing verses of free poetry, the curated echoes of found poetry, or the distilled essence of haiku, poetry becomes a lens through which the world is both seen and experienced anew. So, let your journal be a space where poetry breathes, where emotions and observations are not just noted but celebrated in their most vivid forms.

4.4 The "Stream of Consciousness" Technique

When you're clutching that pen, poised over the eager page of your journal, sometimes the dam holding back your thoughts needs a good, solid crack to let the flow begin. Enter the stream of consciousness technique, a method that's as liberating as throwing open the windows during the first breath of spring. It's about letting your thoughts cascade onto the page in an unbridled flow, unfiltered and raw. This technique isn't just about writing; it's about releasing, exploring the meandering paths of your mind without a map or compass.

Unfiltered Thoughts

Think of your mind as a vast, uncharted wilderness, teeming with thoughts that flit and flutter like leaves in the wind. The stream of consciousness technique is your invitation to capture this wild dance, to let the words spill out in their natural rhythm. It's a process that sidesteps the inner critic, that voice that often hushes your rawest, most genuine expressions. Here, in this space, everything is valid. A memory from childhood, a fleeting sensation, the texture of your morning toast - it all belongs. The beauty of this unfiltered approach lies in its honesty and spontaneity, revealing layers of yourself that structured writing might never uncover.

- Begin with the intention to write freely, without judgment.
- Allow every thought, no matter how mundane or disjointed, to find its way onto the page.

Timed Sessions

Setting a timer might seem counterintuitive to the notion of boundless exploration, but it's a paradoxical key that unlocks deeper creativity. The ticking clock creates a gentle pressure, a reminder that this precious time is dedicated solely to your inner exploration. Five minutes, ten minutes, whatever span feels right, becomes a sanctified interval where the world fades, leaving only you and the page. This boundary, rather than constricting, encourages a concentrated release of thoughts, a focused dive into the stream of your consciousness.

- Choose a duration that feels comfortable, yet slightly challenging.
- Resist the urge to pause or edit; keep the pen moving until the timer signals.

Thematic Streams

While the essence of this technique is unstructured expression, introducing a theme or prompt offers a subtle direction, a current that guides your writing without confining it. Perhaps it's a word, an image, or an emotion that's been lingering at the edge of your thoughts. This focal point serves as a starting gate, a gentle push into the flow. As you write, don't be surprised if your stream meanders away from the initial theme; this divergence is not just allowed but celebrated. It's a journey of discovery, where the unexpected twists and turns often lead to the most profound insights.

- Begin with a theme or prompt that resonates with you at the moment.
- Follow where your thoughts lead, even if they stray from the initial focus.

Reflecting on the Process

After the rush of the stream, the calm waters that follow offer a space for reflection. This isn't about critiquing what you've written but rather observing, noticing patterns, recurring themes, or surprising revelations that emerged. Did certain images or emotions bubble up repeatedly? Did your thoughts take an unexpected direction? This reflection is an integral part of the process, a moment to stand on the banks of your stream of consciousness and ponder the journey. It's here, in the quiet aftermath, that the true value of this technique shines, illuminating the depths of your inner landscape, often revealing gems of creativity and insight nestled within the flow.

- Take time to read over your writing without judgment.
- Note any recurring themes, emotions, or unexpected insights that arise.

In this dance with the pen, where thoughts pirouette and leap across the page in a stream of consciousness, you're not just writing; you're engaging in a dialogue with the deepest parts of yourself. It's a technique that doesn't ask for perfection but for presence, for the courage to explore the untamed wilderness of your mind. So, next time you sit down with your journal, remember, the stream is waiting, ready to carry you on a journey of discovery, one unfiltered word at a time.

4.5 Playing with Perspective: Sketching the Same Object Multiple Times

Imagine your journal as a stage, and each page a scene where the actors, in this case, everyday objects, can perform under different lights, from various angles, and through a spectrum of moods. It's here, in this creative playground, that we challenge the ordinary, urging it to reveal its multitude of faces, each telling a different story. Let's explore how sketching the same object multiple times, under varying perspectives, can not only enhance your artistic skills but also deepen your observational and reflective abilities.

Multiple Angles

Start with something simple, like a coffee mug or a houseplant. Now, instead of sketching it from just one angle, move around it, or rotate it, capturing it from at least three different viewpoints. You could look at it from above, giving it a bird's-eye view, then straight on, and finally from below, offering it a grandeur it might not usually possess. This exercise does more than just hone your sketching skills; it encourages a deeper engagement with the subject, prompting you to notice details and nuances you might have missed at first glance.

- For each angle, note the differences in shape, shadow, and proportion.
- Reflect on how the change in perspective alters the object's story or character.

Changing Scales

Now, play with scale. Sketch your chosen object as tiny as a thimble, then as large as a mountain. This isn't just about stretching your imagination; it's about discovering the essence of the object, what makes it itself regardless of size. Does making it smaller draw attention to its fragility or intricacy? Does enlarging it highlight its strength or simplicity? Through this lens of magnification and reduction, we begin to see the object not just as a static item but as a dynamic entity, capable of growth and transformation.

- Experiment with how detail is portrayed at different scales.
- Consider what aspects of the object become more pronounced or fade away with size changes.

Emotional Perspectives

Objects, much like people, can wear their emotions on their sleeves. Choose an emotion – joy, sorrow, nostalgia, anticipation – and let this mood guide your next set of sketches. Imagine your object as a character in a story filled with this emotion. How would joy change its lines and colors? What shadows would sorrow cast? This approach infuses your sketches with a layer of emotional depth, turning them into visual narratives that speak without words.

- Use colors, lines, and surroundings to convey the chosen emotion.
- Pay attention to how imbuing the object with emotion affects your connection to it.

Comparative Reflection

After you've filled your pages with these varied sketches, take a step back. Lay them out before you, a gallery of perspectives, sizes, and moods, each a different chapter of the same story. Now comes the reflective part, a chance to dive into how these variations change your perception of the object. Did seeing it from a different angle reveal something new? Did changing its scale or infusing it with emotion alter its significance to you? This comparison is not just about artistic growth but about cultivating a mindset open to change and diversity in perspective.

- Jot down your observations and feelings about each version of the object.
- Reflect on what this exercise taught you about perspective, both visually and metaphorically.

In this act of sketching and reflection, we find that even the most mundane objects are worlds unto themselves, brimming with stories waiting to be told. Through the lens of perspective, we learn to see not just with our eyes but with our hearts and minds, opening ourselves to a richer understanding of the world around us. So grab that pen, pick an object, and let the pages of your journal be the canvas for a journey of exploration, one sketch at a time.

4.6 Incorporating Mixed Media

Dabbling in mixed media is like hosting a potluck dinner in your journal; everyone's invited, from the watercolor whispers to the bold statements of acrylics, and even the humble graphite pencil gets a seat at the table. This gathering isn't just about making your pages pop (although that's a delightful side effect); it's about layering different voices, textures, and dimensions to tell your story in a way that's as rich and multifaceted as you are.

Exploring Materials

Consider for a moment the endless materials at your disposal, many of which lie beyond the traditional artist's toolkit. Each medium brings its own unique flavor to the mix:

- **Watercolors** offer a translucence that can mimic the fluidity of emotions or the softness of a remembered dream.
- **Acrylics**, with their bold hues and ability to layer, lend a sense of immediacy and vibrancy.
- **Inks** invite a dance of lines and splatters, perfect for when words fall short or when emotions overflow.
- **Graphite and charcoal** provide a grounding element, their shades of gray sketching the bones upon which colors sing.

The real magic happens when these mediums converge on a single page, their interplay creating a dialogue that's visually and emotionally captivating.

Creative Recycling

Before you toss that newspaper or scrap of ribbon into the recycling bin, consider this: your journal is a sanctuary for the overlooked and the everyday. These materials, rich with texture and story, are ripe for repurposing:

- **Newspaper clippings** can serve as a backdrop, their text weaving a subtle narrative layer or offering a contrast to bold imagery.
- **Fabric scraps** introduce a tactile element, their patterns and textures evoking memories or dreams.
- **Packaging**, with its varied materials and prints, can be transformed into visual accents or thematic elements.

This practice isn't just about aesthetics; it's a nod to the sustainability of creativity, proving that beauty and inspiration can be salvaged from the most mundane sources.

Layering Techniques

The art of layering in mixed media is akin to storytelling; each layer adds depth, context, and intrigue. As you layer, consider:

- **Transparency and opacity**: Play with how much of each layer you allow to show through, using transparency to create depth and opacity to highlight.
- **Texture and pattern**: Combine materials with different textures and patterns for visual interest. A smooth wash of watercolor contrasts beautifully with the roughness of torn paper.
- **Balance and contrast**: Strive for a balance between elements, using contrast to draw the eye and create focal points.

Remember, layering is an intuitive process, a conversation between you and your materials. Trust your instincts and let the page evolve organically.

Thematic Pages

Dedicating pages to a single theme or concept allows for a deep dive into a subject that's close to your heart. This focus can transform your journal into a series of explorations, each page a world unto itself. When approaching thematic pages, consider:

- **Personal symbols**: Identify symbols that hold personal meaning and explore their representation using mixed media.
- **Narratives**: Use a combination of text, imagery, and materials to tell a story or convey an experience.
- **Abstract concepts**: Challenge yourself to represent abstract ideas, such as time, love, or growth, through the interplay of different media.

Creating thematic pages is an invitation to think expansively, to experiment freely, and to express yourself in ways that words alone might not capture. It's a process of discovery, not just of the theme at hand but of your own creative language and how it can evolve when given free rein.

In the realm of mixed media, your journal becomes a canvas for experimentation, a place where different materials and mediums converge to create something greater than the sum of their parts. It's a celebration of diversity, a testament to the richness that comes from combining voices, textures, and stories. So gather your materials, let go of expectations, and allow yourself to play, explore, and create without boundaries.

4.7 The Role of Music in Creative Journaling

There's a secret symphony that plays in the background of our lives, a soundtrack that underscores every moment, every emotion, and every memory. Have you ever noticed how a certain melody can transport you back in time, evoke a long-forgotten memory, or amplify the emotions swirling within you? Music, with its universal language, holds an incredible power to inspire, to comfort, and to awaken the deepest parts of our soul. Now, imagine channeling this power into your journaling practice, using music as a muse to explore the vast landscapes of your inner world.

Music as Muse

Think of a song that stirs something within you, a piece of music that resonates on a level beyond mere enjoyment. It could be the comforting strumming of an acoustic guitar, the haunting melody of a piano piece, or the energetic beats of a dance track. Play this song as you sit down with your journal, letting the music wash over you, seep into you. Pay attention to the emotions it evokes, the memories it summons, or the images it conjures in your mind's eye. Allow these sensations to guide your pen, writing freely, without restraint, letting the music lead your narrative. Whether it's exploring the emotions the song evokes or visually interpreting the music through abstract sketches, let the rhythm, the melody, and the lyrics infuse your entries with a new depth of expression.

Lyric Exploration

Lyrics, with their poetic essence, are ripe for exploration in your journal. Pick a line from a song that speaks to you, a phrase that echoes in the corridors of your mind. Use this line as a springboard for your entry, delving into why it resonates with you, the personal significance it holds, or the story it sparks in your imagination. This exercise not only deepens your connection with the music but also opens up new avenues of reflection and creativity in your journaling. The lyrics become a dialogue, a conversation between you and the song, each line a thread weaving through the fabric of your experiences and emotions.

Soundtrack of Your Life

Every phase of our lives has its own melody, a collection of songs that encapsulate the essence of that time. Creating a "soundtrack" for different periods or events in your life is a dynamic way to document your journey. Start by listing songs that remind you of significant moments—childhood, adolescence, pivotal life events—and alongside each, jot down memories, feelings, and reflections these songs evoke. Accompany these entries with related artwork or narratives, creating a multimedia diary that not only captures your history but also the emotional landscape of each phase. This soundtrack becomes a musical time capsule, each note a key unlocking the chambers of your past.

Musical Backgrounds

The ambiance music creates can significantly influence the tone and theme of your journaling session. Experiment with playing different genres or tempos of music as you write, noting how each affects your creativity and the direction of your entries. A serene instrumental piece might lead to introspective musings, while an upbeat track could inspire lively, energetic reflections. This background music sets the stage for your writing, subtly guiding the mood and flow of your thoughts. It's an experiment in sensory stimulation, exploring how auditory cues can shape the narrative and emotional tone of your journaling practice.

In weaving music into the tapestry of your journaling, you're not just documenting life; you're enriching it with a layer of sonic texture that breathes life into your words. Music becomes a lens through which you view your experiences, a filter that colors your reflections with deeper hues of emotion and meaning. So, let your playlist unfurl, let the melodies seep into your soul, and watch as your journaling practice transforms into a dance of words and music, each entry a duet between your inner world and the universal language of melodies.

4.8 Using Quotes as Journaling Prompts

There's a hidden power in words spoken by others—whether they're lifted from the pages of a beloved book, whispered through the reels of an old film, or penned down by historical figures whose lives paint the canvas of our world. These words, these quotes, carry with them seeds of inspiration, reflection, and sometimes, transformation. Why not invite them into your journaling practice? Let's explore how the wisdom of others can become a catalyst for your own self-discovery and creativity.

Inspirational Words

Imagine stumbling upon a quote that stops you in your tracks, a line so potent it seems to echo the murmurings of your own heart. This resonance is where your journey with the quote begins. It's about more than just admiration; it's about connection. As you weave these words into your journaling, consider the bridge they form between the author's experience and your own. What truths do they unveil about your life, your dreams, your struggles? This exploration can turn a simple quote into a profound journaling session, one that invites introspection and possibly, revelation.

- Choose a quote that resonates with you deeply.
- Write about why it strikes a chord. Is it a reflection of your current state, a reminder of a forgotten truth, or a nudge towards a path you've hesitated to take?

Visual Quote Pages

There's a certain magic in seeing words come to life visually. This is where your journal becomes not just a repository of thoughts but a canvas for artistic expression. Creating a visual page dedicated to a favorite quote can be a deeply personal and creatively fulfilling exercise. Think of integrating calligraphy, surrounding illustrations that capture the essence of the quote, or even a collage that represents its impact on you. This process not only celebrates the quote in a visual format but also embeds its meaning more deeply into your psyche.

- Select a quote and meditate on its imagery, emotion, and message.
- Use colors, drawings, or collage elements to build a page that visually compliments the essence of the quote.

Dialogue with the Quoted

Ever wished you could have a conversation with the minds behind the words that move you? Your journal offers a space to do just that. Writing a dialogue with the author of your chosen quote, or even with the quote itself, opens up a unique avenue for exploration. It's an imaginative exercise that can lead to surprising insights, as you "discuss" the quote's relevance to your life, question its assertions, or even debate its meaning. This process not only deepens your connection with the quote but also encourages a multifaceted reflection on its place in your world.

- Write down the quote, then pen your initial reactions or questions as if speaking directly to its author.
- Continue the conversation, allowing it to flow naturally, exploring different facets of the quote and its impact on you.

Quote Collection

There's something to be said for having a treasure trove of words that inspire, challenge, and comfort you all in one place. Designating a section of your journal for collecting meaningful quotes creates a go-to sanctuary of wisdom. Over time, this collection becomes a reflection of your journey, each quote a milestone or a beacon of light during different chapters of your life. Revisiting these pages can offer solace, motivation, and perhaps a new perspective on quotes that have grown alongside you.

- Dedicate a section of your journal to quotes. This can be at the beginning, end, or interspersed between your entries.
- Whenever a quote strikes you, add it to your collection along with a note about why it matters to you at that moment.

In weaving quotes into the fabric of your journaling practice, you're doing more than just recording words; you're engaging in a dialogue with the collective wisdom of humanity. You're allowing the experiences, dreams, and reflections of others to mirror your own, creating a layered tapestry of introspection and inspiration. Each quote, each page, becomes a steppingstone in your journey of self-discovery, inviting you to see the world, and yourself, through a kaleidoscope of perspectives.

4.9 Designing Your Own Journaling Prompts

Creating your own journaling prompts is like setting out a picnic in your favorite part of the mental landscape. Sometimes, the pre-packaged questions don't quite suit your taste or the occasion. That's where crafting personalized prompts comes into play, tailored to resonate with your current musings, desires, or challenges. This exercise is not just about filling pages; it's about curating questions that tug at the threads of your thoughts, unraveling insights you might not have discovered otherwise.

Prompt Creation

Start by reflecting on areas of your life that are currently under the spotlight - perhaps it's personal growth, creativity, relationships, or career aspirations. What questions keep circling around, seeking your attention? Begin with these. For instance, if creativity is your focus, you might ask, "What's one creative fear I want to overcome?" The beauty here lies in specificity; the more precise your prompts, the deeper you can dive.

- Reflect on areas of your life craving exploration.
- Formulate questions that tap directly into these themes.
- Aim for specificity to encourage depth in your responses.

Prompt Sharing

Imagine a garden where, instead of flowers, it's ideas that bloom and cross-pollinate. Sharing your custom prompts with a journaling community or friends who also journal can spark this kind of vibrant exchange. It's a practice that not only enriches your own experience but also weaves a tapestry of connection and mutual inspiration. You might discover new perspectives on a familiar question or find that your prompt has been the key to unlocking someone else's creative block.

- Share prompts in online communities or with journaling buddies.
- Engage with the responses and reflections your prompts inspire in others.
- Embrace the communal growth and inspiration that arises from shared exploration.

Themed Prompt Lists

Creating a list of themed prompts acts as a compass, guiding you through the exploration of a particular theme over days or weeks. This approach allows you to layer your insights, building a rich and nuanced understanding of the theme. You might choose a theme like 'Transition', crafting prompts that explore the facets of change, such as, "What change am I resisting and why?" or "How do I feel in moments of transition, and what does that teach me?"

- Select a theme that resonates with your current life phase or interests.
- Craft a series of prompts that explore various aspects of this theme.
- Use these prompts sequentially to deepen your exploration and understanding.

Reflective Prompts

The heart of journaling often lies in those quiet moments of self-reflection, where we turn the mirror inward to examine our thoughts, feelings, and aspirations. Incorporating reflective prompts into your journaling practice invites a journey inward, one that can illuminate paths of growth and self-awareness. These prompts might ask you to confront your fears, celebrate your strengths, or ponder the future. For example, "What part of myself have I been neglecting, and how can I nurture it moving forward?"

- Focus on prompts that encourage introspection and self-dialogue.
- Tackle themes of personal growth, fears, achievements, and dreams.
- Allow these prompts to be starting points for deeper exploration, without expectation of definitive answers.

In curating your personal collection of prompts, you're not just setting the stage for routine journal entries; you're crafting gateways to self-discovery, each question a key unlocking deeper understanding and insight. So, grab that pen, and let's turn those thoughts into a dialogue, one prompt at a time.

4.10 The Blank Space: Leaving Room for Future Thoughts

In the tapestry of your journaling adventure, imagine each entry, each doodle, and each musing as vibrant threads weaving through the fabric of your pages. Now, picture deliberately leaving patches of this tapestry untouched, blank spaces scattered amidst the color and chaos. These areas of intentional emptiness are not oversight; they are opportunities, silent invitations for future creativity, reflection, and growth.

Intentional Emptiness

The act of leaving room in your journal is akin to planting a garden and leaving patches of soil bare, reserved for seeds yet to be discovered. These blank spaces in your journal are fertile ground for the thoughts, ideas, and inspirations that have yet to take root. They stand as open doors to future self-expressions, waiting for the right moment, the right feeling, or the right experience to fill them. This practice encourages a mindset that views the journal not as a static record but as a living, evolving entity.

- Think of these spaces as breathing room for your creativity.
- Use them to invite spontaneity into your journaling practice.

Space for Growth

Just as we, as individuals, are ever-changing and evolving, so too should our journals reflect this dynamism. By intentionally incorporating blank spaces within your pages, you're acknowledging that growth and change are not only inevitable but welcome. These spaces symbolize the understanding that our future selves will have new insights, experiences, and artistic inclinations that deserve a place within our journals. They remind us that our journey is ongoing and that our evolution as individuals is a beautiful, never-ending process.

- See these spaces as placeholders for future versions of yourself.
- Allow them to reflect the understanding that change is a constant and valuable part of life.

Adding Over Time

The true magic of these intentional blank spaces unfolds as you revisit them over time, each addition layering new meaning and depth upon the page. Today, it might be a quote that struck a chord with your current self; tomorrow, a sketch inspired by a dream; next month, a photo that captures a fleeting moment of joy. This practice of returning and adding transforms each page into a palimpsest, a historical document of your personal growth and changing perspectives. It's a visual and tangible record of how you've evolved, each entry a thread in the larger narrative of your life.

- Periodically revisit these spaces with fresh eyes and new experiences.
- Treat each addition as a building block in the ongoing story of your self-discovery.

Reflecting on the Journey

As you flip through your journal, these pages—once blank and now brimming with layers of thoughts, sketches, and memories—serve as milestones on your journey. They offer a unique perspective on how far you've come, not just in your artistic or writing abilities, but in your capacity for introspection and growth. This reflection is not merely an exercise in nostalgia; it's an affirmation of your evolution, a testament to the depth and richness of your journey. It reminds you that growth often comes in unexpected moments and that your journal is a faithful companion, bearing witness to this beautiful, messy, and utterly human process of becoming.

- View these evolving pages as a celebration of your journey.
- Recognize the value in each layer, each addition, as a step in your ongoing evolution.

As we close this exploration of leaving room for future thoughts, remember that your journal is more than just a collection of pages; it's a canvas for your life's work. The blank spaces you leave today are invitations for tomorrow's creativity, reflections, and revelations. They are a testament to the belief that growth is perpetual, and change, though uncertain, is a beautiful certainty. With this mindset, your journal becomes not just a record of who you were but a map guiding you toward who you are becoming. As we move forward, let's carry with us the understanding that every blank space, every untouched corner of our journals, holds the potential for new beginnings, new insights, and an ever-deepening connection with ourselves.

Chapter 5

The Urban Jungle Notebook

Picture this: a concrete jungle, where the rush of traffic melds with the rustle of leaves in the park. It's where skyscrapers meet the sky, and amidst this bustling metropolis, nature thrives in pockets of green, often unnoticed by hurried passersby. This chapter is your guide to rediscovering these hidden gems, transforming the way you see, think about, and interact with nature in urban settings. It's not about escaping the city but embracing its unique blend of natural beauty. Let's peel back the layers of asphalt and concrete to reveal the thriving ecosystems that make city life a bit more breathable.

5.1 Urban Nature Spots

Finding nature in the city is like discovering secret passages in a well-trodden castle. It requires a bit of curiosity and a willingness to look beyond the obvious. Start with:

- **Parks and Gardens**: More than just picnic spots, these are ecosystems teeming with life. Pay attention to the variety of plants, the insects bustling about, and the birds that call these places home.
- **Rooftop Gardens**: Ascend above street level to find gardens that defy gravity. These spaces not only offer a respite from urban hustle but also contribute to biodiversity and reduce building energy consumption.
- **Greenways and River Walks**: These corridors of greenery are vital for wildlife, offering migration paths and habitats. They're also perfect for human wanderers seeking a moment of tranquility.

On your next urban expedition, keep an eye out for these havens. Take note of how nature adapts to city life, flourishing in the crevices of our urban landscape.

Micro Observations

The devil, or in this case, the beauty, is in the details. It's about tuning into the micro-environments that exist underfoot or overhead, often overlooked in our daily rush. Consider:

- **Cracks in the Sidewalk**: A tiny plant pushing through concrete is a testament to nature's resilience. Document its growth, and you'll find a narrative of survival and persistence.
- **Insects on the Move**: From industrious ants marching to pollinators visiting urban flowers, insects are the unsung heroes of city ecology. Observing them can offer insights into the health and diversity of urban nature.

These observations remind us that nature exists all around us, operating on a scale that often requires us to slow down and look closer.

Seasonal Changes

Cities have seasons too, marked not just by the changing weather but by the transformation of urban nature spaces. Observing these changes offers a deeper connection to the natural rhythms of life amid the concrete:

- **Deciduous Trees in Parks**: Watch as their leaves change color, drop, and regrow, a visible marker of the passing seasons.
- **Annual Flower Plantings**: Many cities plant flowers seasonally. Documenting these changes can add a colorful dimension to your journal.
- **Wildlife Behavior**: Note how the behavior of urban wildlife shifts with the seasons, from nesting birds in spring to squirrels gathering food in fall.

These seasonal shifts offer a backdrop to our lives, a reminder of nature's cycles playing out in the heart of the city.

Sketching Urban Wildlife

Sketching is a powerful way to engage with urban wildlife, requiring you to observe closely and appreciate the nuances of each creature's existence. Here's how to get started:

- **Quick Sketches**: Animals in the city are often on the move. Practice quick sketches that capture the essence of their movement and form.
- **Feathered Friends**: Birds in city parks can be excellent subjects. Note their varied species, behaviors, and how they interact with the urban environment.
- **Squirrels, Rabbits, and More**: These common city dwellers have adapted well to urban life. Sketching them can offer fascinating insights into urban ecology.

These sketches serve as a visual diary of the wildlife that shares our urban spaces, enriching our understanding of city ecosystems.

By turning our gaze to the natural elements that flourish in our cities, we not only deepen our connection to the environment but also cultivate a sense of wonder and appreciation for the resilient nature that exists amidst the urban sprawl. Whether it's through jotting down observations, sketching a fleeting moment, or simply pausing to observe, the act of documenting urban nature transforms our relationship with the city. It reminds us that even in the most unexpected places, life finds a way to thrive, offering moments of beauty and tranquility in the midst of our busy lives.

5.2 Drawing Nature When You Think You Can't

In the heart of the city, amidst the hustle and the endless hum of activity, the thought of drawing nature might seem like a distant dream. Maybe you've convinced yourself that you can't draw, or perhaps the urban landscape seems devoid of natural beauty at first glance. But here's a little secret: every one of us has the ability to capture the essence of nature on paper, and the city is teeming with life waiting to be noticed and sketched. Let's unwrap this gift together, step by step.

Simplified Shapes and Forms

Look around you; nature in the city is not as hidden as you might think. A tree silhouetted against a high-rise building, a pigeon perched on a lamppost, or even weeds breaking through the pavement—all are candidates for your sketchbook. The key is to break down what you see into the simplest shapes and forms. A leaf could start as an oval, a tree trunk as a rectangle, and a bird as a combination of circles. It's not about capturing every detail but rather the basic essence of the subject. This approach makes the process less daunting for beginners and opens up a world where anything can be sketched with a few simple lines.

- Start with broad, simple shapes to capture the essence of your subject.
- Practice this technique with everyday objects to build confidence.

Emphasizing Observation Over Accuracy

One common hurdle in sketching nature, especially for those who believe they lack artistic talent, is the pressure to create something 'accurate'. Let's shift that focus towards observation instead. When you look at a flower, notice its color, the way the light falls on its petals, or how it sways in the breeze. These observations are what you'll bring to your sketch, not an exact botanical illustration. This shift not only relieves the pressure but also connects you more deeply with your subject, making the act of sketching a form of mindfulness.

- Let go of the need for perfection and focus on the process of observing.
- Use your sketches to document how you see the world, not to replicate it perfectly.

Using References

Sometimes, direct observation might not be possible, or you might want to practice drawing a specific aspect of nature not readily available in your urban setting. This is where references come into play. Photos from a recent trip to the park, images from a nature magazine, or even online resources can serve as valuable tools for practice and inspiration. They allow you to keep practicing even when you can't be out in nature, ensuring that your sketching skills continue to grow.

- Collect images of nature scenes, plants, and animals that inspire you.
- Practice sketching from these references, paying attention to shape, form, and texture.

Sharing and Reflecting

Finally, one of the most enriching aspects of drawing nature is sharing your sketches with others. This doesn't mean you need to mount an art exhibition; it can be as simple as showing a friend or posting in an online community. Sharing your work opens the door to feedback, encouragement, and connection with fellow nature enthusiasts. Moreover, reflecting on your sketches, either on your own or with others, can be a profound source of joy and growth. It allows you to see your progress over time, to appreciate your unique perspective, and to find joy in the simple act of creation, irrespective of the outcome.

- Share your sketches with friends or online communities dedicated to nature sketching or journaling.
- Reflect on your sketches regularly to appreciate your growth and the beauty of your unique perspective.

In weaving these threads together—breaking nature down into simple shapes, focusing on observation, using references, and sharing your journey—you'll find that drawing nature isn't just about creating art. It's about connecting more deeply with the world around you, finding beauty in the everyday, and discovering the joy of expressing your perspective on paper. So grab that pencil, and let's start sketching the vibrant tapestry of urban nature that surrounds us.

5.3 Mindfulness Exercises Outdoors

In the canvas of the urban environment, where concrete meets sky, there's a symphony of natural moments waiting to be discovered. It's here, in the interplay of shadow and light, sound and silence, that we find a rich ground for mindfulness exercises. These practices offer a bridge, connecting our inner world with the external environment, allowing us to draw from the well of present experiences to enrich our journaling journey.

Nature as a Mindfulness Tool

Imagine stepping outside, where the air holds a crispness that speaks of the changing seasons, and the city's heartbeat creates a backdrop to your own rhythm. This setting is ripe for mindfulness practices. One such practice is **mindful walking**, where each step becomes an act of awareness, feeling the ground beneath your feet, noticing the sway of trees in the breeze, and observing the dance of light as it filters through the leaves. Another practice is to **focus on the sounds of nature**, letting the urban symphony fade into the background as you tune into the chorus of birds, the whisper of wind, or the patter of rain on pavement. These exercises ground you in the moment, turning the ordinary into the extraordinary.

- Find a green space where you can walk slowly, paying attention to your senses.
- Sit quietly in a park, close your eyes, and focus solely on the natural sounds around you.

Journaling Post-Mindfulness

After engaging in these mindfulness exercises, your senses are heightened, and your connection to the present moment deepened. This is a golden opportunity to bring out your journal. With fresh observations, feelings, and insights swirling within, let the words flow onto the page. This immediate transition from mindfulness to journaling captures the essence of your experience with vivid clarity. It's not just about documenting what you saw or heard but expressing how these moments resonated with you, both emotionally and physically.

- Keep your journal handy during your mindfulness exercises for immediate reflection.
- Write about not just what you observed but how it made you feel, exploring the connection between your external and internal experiences.

Sensory Details

Incorporating sensory details into your journal entries transforms them from mere observations to immersive experiences. As you reflect on your mindfulness practice, delve into the specifics: the texture of the bark you brushed against, the scent of rain on concrete, the chorus of city birds at dusk. These details act as anchors, pulling the reader (and your future self) back into the moment with you. They enrich your journal, making it a vibrant tapestry of lived experiences rather than a simple log of events.

- Describe each sense in detail: what you saw, heard, smelled, touched, and even tasted.
- Use descriptive language to bring these sensory experiences to life on the page.

Gratitude for Nature

Ending each outdoor mindfulness session with a journal entry expressing gratitude for the natural world does more than just cap off your practice; it cultivates a mindset of appreciation and wonder. It's easy to take the everyday beauty of our surroundings for granted, especially in the hustle of city life. By consciously acknowledging the gifts nature offers us, even in the most urban of environments, we foster a deeper connection to the world around us and a greater appreciation for our place within it. This gratitude becomes a wellspring of positivity, influencing our perspective and interactions with our environment.

- List specific elements of nature you encountered and why you're grateful for them.
- Reflect on how these natural encounters impact your well-being and outlook on life.

In weaving these threads together—mindful observation, immediate journaling, sensory exploration, and gratitude—we not only deepen our journaling practice but also our connection to the world around us. Nature, even within the urban sprawl, offers a myriad of moments ripe for mindfulness, waiting to be discovered and documented. So next time you step outside, let the city's natural rhythm guide you into a state of awareness, and let this awareness fill the pages of your journal, creating a rich narrative of your encounters with the world.

5.4 Crafting Your Portable Nature Journaling Kit

Imagine stepping out your door, ready to capture the whisper of leaves and the symphony of the city's hidden natural corners. Your first step on this path of urban exploration and artistic endeavor begins with assembling your trusty sidekick: a nature journaling kit tailored just for you. This kit isn't merely a collection of tools; it's your passport to discovery, a way to ensure you're always ready when inspiration strikes, whether it's a sunbeam filtering through an alleyway or a hawk circling above a skyscraper.

Essential Supplies for Your Kit

At its core, your kit cradles the essentials:

- **A Durable Journal**: Choose one that can withstand a bit of rough handling, as urban adventures can sometimes lead you off the beaten path. Water-resistant covers and thick pages that don't bleed are your best friends here.
- **Pencils and Pens**: A variety of pencils for sketching and pens that promise no smudges or leaks will keep your observations intact.
- **A Small Watercolor Set**: Compact and portable, it lets you bring the city's colors to life right on your page.

- **Portable Stool or Mat**: Sometimes, the perfect spot for your journaling is not a convenient bench but a quiet corner in a park. A lightweight, foldable stool or a small mat gives you the freedom to set up anywhere.

This foundation supports your journey, ensuring you have the basics at your fingertips to bring your urban nature explorations to vibrant life.

Customizing Your Kit

Your kit should feel like an extension of yourself, versatile enough to adapt to your curiosity and needs:

- **Binoculars for Bird Watching**: If your heart soars with the birds, a compact pair of binoculars can bring the details into focus, enriching your sketches and notes.
- **Magnifying Glass**: For the tiny wonders—a flower bud or an intricate insect—a magnifying glass reveals worlds within worlds, adding depth to your observations.
- **Reference Books or Apps**: Sometimes, the flora and fauna that catch your eye will be mysteries waiting to be solved. A pocket field guide or an app can help identify and understand your discoveries.

As you grow in your journaling journey, your kit will evolve too, molding itself to fit your interests and the unique blend of nature that thrives in your urban environment.

Minimizing Environmental Impact

While we venture into nature's nooks within the city, our footsteps should tread lightly, respecting the delicate balance around us:

- **Practice Leave No Trace Principles**: Keep your impact minimal. This means taking only photos and leaving only footprints, ensuring the scenes you capture stay pristine for fellow explorers and city dwellers.
- **Sustainable Materials**: Opt for a journal made of recycled paper, pencils from sustainable sources, and reusable water containers for your paints. Every choice is a step towards a greener, more mindful engagement with our environment.

This mindful approach enriches your practice, aligning your creative exploration with a commitment to preserving the beauty that inspires it.

Inspiration on the Go

The best moments often catch us by surprise, in the fleeting glow of sunset against glass or the sudden appearance of a fox on a quiet street. Keeping your kit ready and within reach ensures you're always prepared to capture these whispers of urban nature:

- **Pack Light**: Your kit should be light enough to carry without a second thought. This encourages spontaneity, allowing you to grab it and go whenever the mood strikes or the opportunity arises.
- **Routine Checks**: Regularly replenish and review your kit. Make sure your pens haven't run dry, your watercolor pans are full, and your journal has plenty of blank pages waiting to be filled.

Having your kit at the ready means never missing an opportunity to document the unexpected beauty around you, turning everyday moments into a canvas for your creativity and reflection.

In crafting your nature journaling kit, you're preparing not just a bag of tools but a treasure chest of possibilities. It's your ally in the quest for beauty amidst the bustle, a constant reminder of the layers of life and art waiting to be discovered in the urban landscape. With your kit by your side, every walk becomes an adventure, every observation a masterpiece, and every moment a chance to see the world anew.

5.5 Weather Patterns and Your Mood

The dance of clouds above, the whisper of an impending storm, the warmth of the sun parting the grey – the city's skies tell a tale not just of coming rain or shine but of our inner weathers too. Here, where concrete meets the vast expanse of the sky, the weather plays its tune on the strings of our emotions and perceptions. Let's explore how the rhythm of urban weather shapes our days and finds its echo in the pages of our journals.

Observing Weather

Begin with the simple act of watching the sky. Notice how the weather shifts, from the first light of dawn to the velvety cloak of night. Keep a weather eye on:

- The shape and movement of clouds, noting their textures and patterns.
- The play of light, how it changes the look and feel of the city.
- Sudden weather changes, like a storm rolling in or a fog descending.

This daily observation becomes a practice in mindfulness, connecting you with the environment and its ever-changing moods.

Weather and Emotions

Have you ever noticed how a rainy day might cloak you in introspection or how a sunny morning can lift your spirits? The weather outside often mirrors our internal landscapes. To dive deeper:

- On a stormy day, write about the emotions that surface. Is there a sense of anticipation, a touch of melancholy, or perhaps an unexpected calm?

- During a spell of sunshine, reflect on the shifts in your mood. Does the lightness outside seep into your thoughts and feelings?
- Explore how extreme weather, like a heatwave or a snowstorm, affects your energy and outlook.

This exploration offers insights into how deeply intertwined our inner lives are with the external world, highlighting the weather's subtle yet profound impact on our emotional well-being.

Creative Weather Descriptions

Describing weather in your journal can transcend mere observation, turning into an art form that paints the atmosphere of your days. To capture the essence:

- Use metaphors and similes to bring weather conditions to life. A day might not just be hot but "as if the city were wrapped in a thick, woolen blanket, stifling and heavy."
- Incorporate sensory details. How does the air smell before rain? What's the texture of a foggy morning?
- Reflect on the weather's impact on the cityscape. How does rain change the way the streets look, sound, and feel?

This creative endeavor not only enriches your journaling practice but also sharpens your writing skills, offering a fresh lens through which to view the familiar.

Weather Predictions

Embrace the role of an urban meteorologist, making your weather predictions based on observations. This playful exercise can be both engaging and enlightening. Here's how:

- Note the signs that hint at changing weather, like a shift in wind direction or the formation of certain cloud types.
- Write down your predictions for the next day or week. Will it rain? Will there be a sudden drop in temperature?
- Compare your predictions with actual outcomes. Over time, you might find patterns in your observations, honing your ability to read the city's weather signals.

This activity not only adds an element of fun to your journaling but also deepens your connection with the natural rhythms of the urban environment, bridging the gap between the city's pulse and the broader tapestry of the natural world around it.

In turning our gaze skyward and attuning ourselves to the whispers of the wind and the tales of the clouds, we find a mirror for our moods and a muse for our journaling. The weather, with its ever-changing face, reminds us of the flux within and around us, urging us to capture these moments in our journals. Through observation, reflection, and creative expression, we weave the external and internal into a narrative that is uniquely ours, marked by the rhythm of the seasons and the beat of the city's heart.

5.6 Urban Wildlife Observations

The urban landscape, often perceived as a domain dominated by steel and concrete, is in reality a vibrant mosaic of life. Amidst the hustle and bustle of city life, a diverse array of wildlife has adeptly carved out niches for survival and thrival. From the fleeting glimpses of birds weaving through skyscrapers to the more grounded presence of urban foxes navigating alleyways, the city is alive with non-human narratives waiting to be discovered and documented.

Wildlife in the City

Venture into this untamed urban wilderness with eyes wide open, and you'll find a world teeming with life that often goes unnoticed. The air is filled with the songs of birds, from the melodious calls of the morning dove to the spirited chatter of the sparrow. Look closer at the shadows cast by foliage, and you might spot the scurry of a squirrel or the poised elegance of a cat on the prowl. Even the seemingly desolate nooks of buildings become stages for the dance of insects, from the industrious ant to the solitary bee seeking urban blooms. This rich tapestry of urban wildlife not only adds a layer of wonder to the cityscape but also serves as a reminder of nature's adaptability and resilience.

Documenting Encounters

Capturing these encounters in your journal transforms fleeting moments into lasting impressions. Start by noting the date, time, and location of your observation, anchoring your encounter in the here and now. Describe the species observed, paying attention to its appearance, behaviors, and any interactions with its environment or other animals. Were they foraging, nesting, or perhaps engaging in a territorial display? These notes not only serve as a record of urban biodiversity but also as a personal reflection on the encounter. How did it make you feel? What thoughts or questions did it evoke? This reflective practice deepens your connection to the urban wild, fostering a sense of kinship and curiosity.

Ethical Observations

As urban naturalists, our excitement to engage with wildlife must be tempered with respect for their autonomy and well-being. Always observe from a distance that does not disturb or alter their behavior. Resist the temptation to feed wildlife, as this can lead to dependency and conflict. Remember, we are guests in their urban territory, and our observations should leave no trace on their daily routines. This mindful approach ensures that our curiosity contributes to a harmonious coexistence, where human and non-human lives intersect with mutual respect.

Sketching Techniques

Bringing wildlife encounters to life through sketches adds a dynamic dimension to your journaling. Embrace simplicity and speed; quick sketches capture the essence of a moment, reflecting the vitality and movement inherent in urban wildlife. Start with light, swift strokes to outline basic shapes and postures, gradually adding details as the scene or memory allows. Don't worry about perfection. The value lies in the act of observation and the emotional resonance of the sketch. Celebrate mismatches and quirks in your drawings as reflections of the unpredictable and spirited nature of urban wildlife. Through these artistic endeavors, your journal becomes a visual and textual ode to the city's wild heart, a testament to the beauty and diversity that thrives amidst the concrete.

In the heart of the city, where human and non-human worlds intertwine, wildlife observations offer a portal to a parallel universe brimming with stories, struggles, and splendor. By documenting these encounters, we not only create a record of urban biodiversity but also weave ourselves into the fabric of the larger ecological narrative. Our journals become bridges, connecting us to the myriad lives that share our urban spaces, enriching our understanding and appreciation of the world around us. Through ethical observation and creative expression, we pay homage to the resilience and beauty of urban wildlife, finding wonder in the wildness that flourishes in the cracks of our cityscapes.

5.7   Plant Growth Tracking

Navigating the bustling streets of the city, amidst the cacophony of daily life, it's easy to overlook the silent, steadfast growth of the green companions that pepper our urban landscape. Yet, these plants, whether they perch on a windowsill, flourish in a park, or break through a crack in the pavement, narrate a story of resilience and beauty. Dedicating a section of your nature journal to tracking the growth of these plants offers not just a window into the botanical life thriving in concrete crevices but also serves as a metaphor for personal evolution and change.

Choosing a Plant Subject

Initiating your botanical journey begins with selecting a plant or group of plants to observe. This choice could be as simple as a potted friend on your windowsill or as communal as a tree in your local park. What matters is the connection you feel to this living entity and your curiosity about its life cycle. Consider plants with visible changes over time, such as flowering species or deciduous trees, to maximize the observational experience. Your chosen plant becomes a focal point, a living subject through which you can explore the interplay between nature and urban life.

- Opt for a plant easily accessible for regular observation.

- Look for species with noticeable growth or changes, enhancing the tracking experience.

Regular Observation Entries

With your plant subject chosen, the next step is integrating regular observation entries into your journaling routine. These entries are snapshots in time, documenting the subtle shifts in growth, the emergence of buds, or the changing of leaves. Each entry should note the date, time, and weather conditions, providing context to your observations. Describe the plant's current state, including height, leaf count, or any signs of flowering. Over time, these entries weave a detailed narrative of growth, offering insights into the plant's life cycle and its interaction with the urban environment.

- Make observations a part of your daily or weekly routine for consistency.
- Note environmental conditions alongside plant changes to track the impact of weather and seasons.

Photographic Documentation

Complementing your written observations with photographs brings a dynamic visual element to your plant growth tracking. Photos capture the beauty and detail of changes over time, from the unfurling of a leaf to the full bloom of a flower. They serve as vivid reminders of moments you've shared with your plant subject, adding depth to your journal. When incorporating photos, consider using instant film for a vintage feel or printing digital photos if you're tech-savvy. Arrange these images alongside your entries, creating a rich, visual chronicle of your plant's journey through the seasons.

- Capture photos from the same angle for consistency.
- Use photos to highlight details or changes difficult to convey through text alone.

Reflecting on Growth

The act of tracking plant growth in your journal transcends mere observation; it becomes a reflective practice, mirroring your own growth and change. As you document the lifecycle of your chosen plant, draw parallels to your personal journey. Consider how you, like the plant, have adapted to your urban environment, faced challenges, and grown over time. Reflect on the lessons learned from your plant subject, such as resilience, patience, and the beauty of change. This reflection deepens your connection to both the natural world and your inner self, highlighting the intertwined paths of personal and botanical growth.

- Use your plant's growth stages as metaphors for personal milestones or challenges.
- Reflect on your observations and feelings, exploring the personal significance of the changes you've documented.

In tracking the growth of plants within the urban landscape, your journal becomes more than a collection of observations; it transforms into a living document that celebrates the cycle of life, resilience, and beauty inherent in both nature and ourselves. Through this practice, we're reminded of the power of attention, the joy of connection, and the profound lessons that even the smallest of urban plants can teach us.

5.8 Nature Journaling as a Group Activity

Stepping into the great outdoors, even if it's the green patch amidst urban sprawl, with a group of like-minded individuals, transforms the solitary act of journaling into a collective adventure. It's in these shared moments that nature reveals its lessons not just through the lens of personal introspection but within the dynamics of community and shared experiences. This section sheds light on how to bring people together for nature journaling outings, enrich every participant's experience, and foster a community that thrives on mutual appreciation for nature's wonders.

Organizing Group Outings

Gathering a group for a nature journaling excursion requires a dash of planning and a sprinkle of spontaneity. Start by scouting out locations that promise a blend of accessibility and natural diversity. City parks, botanical gardens, or riverwalks offer a canvas ripe for exploration. When planning:

- **Accessibility is Key**: Choose spots that are easily accessible for everyone, considering public transportation and parking availability.
- **Varied Skill Levels**: Remember, the group might span from novices to seasoned journalers. Select locations that offer a range of stimuli, ensuring everyone finds inspiration.
- **Plan B**: Weather can be fickle, especially in urban settings. Have an indoor option in mind, like a conservatory or museum with natural exhibits, ensuring your outing is foolproof.

Shared Observations

Once the group is assembled, and pencils are poised, encourage everyone to share their observations aloud. This exchange of perspectives:

- **Broadens Horizons**: Hearing what others notice, which might have slipped by your observation, broadens your own perception of the natural world.
- **Skill Exchange**: More experienced journalers can share tips with beginners, fostering a learning environment that elevates everyone's experience.
- **Inspiration Through Diversity**: The variety in observation and journaling styles sparks creativity, pushing everyone to experiment with new techniques or perspectives.

Group Reflections

After a period of individual exploration and sketching, gathering the group for a reflection session enriches the experience. This can take place on a quiet spot on-site or back at a café, where the group can unwind and share. During these sessions:

- **Share Pages**: If comfortable, let everyone show a page from their journal. It's not about critique but about celebrating each person's unique way of seeing and documenting nature.
- **Discuss Discoveries**: Talk about what surprised you or what you learned. Was there a plant you couldn't identify? Maybe someone else knows it.
- **Emotional Impact**: Reflect on how the outing made you feel. Did reconnecting with nature uplift your spirits? Sharing these emotional impacts deepens the group's bond.

Building a Community

The culmination of these group outings is the formation of a community, a tribe bound by a shared love for nature and journaling. This community becomes a source of:

- **Ongoing Support**: Having a group offers motivation to continue journaling, encouraging each other through creative slumps or celebrating milestones.
- **Collective Wisdom**: The pooled knowledge and experiences of the group become a reservoir of wisdom for all its members, enriching each person's understanding and appreciation of nature.
- **Inspiration and Accountability**: Regular meet-ups and sharing sessions keep the momentum going, providing both inspiration and a gentle nudge to keep journaling.

In this vibrant community, journaling transforms from a solitary activity into a shared journey, where each member contributes to a collective narrative of nature appreciation. It's here, in the laughter shared over smudged sketches or the collective awe at a newly discovered plant, that journaling becomes more than just an act of documentation—it becomes a way of connecting, learning, and growing together.

5.9 Nature's Impact on Personal Growth

Gazing out into the cityscape, where green spaces breathe life into the concrete expanse, it's easy to overlook the profound lessons nature imparts. Yet, for those who pause to listen, nature's whispers offer invaluable insights into resilience, adaptability, and the intricate web of interconnectedness. This part of our journey invites you to reflect on how your regular encounters with nature, documented meticulously in your journal, serve as catalysts for personal transformation.

Personal Reflections

Reflecting on your interactions with nature, consider how these moments have shaped your perspective on mindfulness, creativity, and overall well-being. Each leaf sketched, each bird's song noted, and each weather pattern observed is more than just an entry; it's a step towards a more mindful existence. These reflections reveal nature's subtle yet powerful influence on our inner growth, encouraging a deeper connection with the present moment, nurturing our creative spirits, and enhancing our emotional and physical well-being.

- Reflect on specific entries that marked a turning point in your appreciation for nature.
- Consider the role of these nature encounters in cultivating a more mindful approach to daily life.

Lessons from Nature

Nature, in its boundless wisdom, teaches invaluable lessons on resilience—how to bend without breaking, adaptability—the art of thriving in ever-changing conditions, and interconnectedness—the understanding that we are part of a larger whole. Documenting these lessons in your journal not only immortalizes them but also integrates them into your personal philosophy.

- Identify and document instances where nature's resilience mirrored your personal challenges and how you overcame them.
- Reflect on how nature's adaptability has inspired you to embrace change more openly.

Setting Intentions

With the insights gleaned from your nature journaling, setting intentions becomes a grounded exercise in aligning your personal growth with the rhythms and lessons of the natural world. Whether it's aspiring to embody the resilience of a city tree or the adaptability of urban wildlife, these intentions guide your path towards personal development, harmonizing with nature's cycles.

- Use your journal to set personal intentions inspired by your observations and reflections on nature.
- Consider how these intentions can be woven into your daily life, mirroring the natural patterns you've documented.

Sharing Your Journey

The journey of personal growth, enriched by the lessons of nature, gains even more depth when shared. Whether through blogging, social media posts, or community presentations, sharing your journey invites others to explore their relationship with nature. It's an opportunity to inspire, to connect, and to foster a collective appreciation for the natural world, even within the urban jungle.

- Share stories from your journal that highlight personal growth inspired by nature.
- Offer insights on how others can embark on their own journey of nature-inspired personal development.

In weaving these threads together—reflection, lessons from nature, intention setting, and sharing—your nature journaling practice becomes more than just a hobby; it's a transformative tool, guiding you towards a deeper understanding of yourself and the world around you. Through this process, we discover that nature, even in its most subdued urban manifestations, holds the keys to profound personal growth and well-being.

As we close this section, we're reminded that the act of journaling, particularly about the natural world around us, is not just an exercise in observation but a doorway to deeper self-awareness and connection. It's a practice that continually teaches us, inspires us, and reminds us of the beauty and resilience inherent in both nature and ourselves. Looking ahead, we carry these lessons with us, ready to explore new horizons and uncover further insights into our relationship with the world and the myriad ways it shapes our journey through life.

Thank you for purchasing this book. If you have found it helpful, please go to Amazon and write a brief review. This would be so appreciated and will give others an idea of what this book is all about.

And please be looking for other books in this series that we will be publishing in the very near future.

Your input will be most appreciated.

Nick and Nora

Chapter 6

Embracing Imperfection in Your Journal

Picture this: a pristine journal laid out before you, its untouched pages gleaming under the light, beckoning for your thoughts, sketches, and dreams. Yet, there's a hitch – the fear of making that first irreversible mark. It's like standing at the edge of a diving board for the first time, the water below promising a thrilling adventure yet the height paralyzing. This chapter is your gentle nudge, or rather, your enthusiastic push into the pool of journaling, where the water is fine, and perfection is not the goal. Let's splash around in the possibilities that come with embracing imperfection in your journal.

6.1 Perfection is Not the Goal

Remember, your journal is not a museum exhibit awaiting critical eyes; it's more like your cozy living room where you can kick off your shoes, be yourself, and make a mess. It's about the process, the act of creating, reflecting, and expressing, not about crafting a masterpiece on every page. So, if your handwriting looks like a doctor's prescription pad or your sketches resemble abstract art only you understand, you're doing it right. Your journal is a judgment-free zone.

Starting with Imperfection

Here's a thought: why not start your journal with a mistake on purpose? Scribble something on the first page, spill a bit of coffee, or let your pen doodle aimlessly. This deliberate imperfection sets the tone for a space where mistakes aren't just tolerated; they're welcomed. It's a reminder that this journal is yours to explore, without the pressure of perfection.

Using Pages for Practice

Reserve the last few pages of your journal as a sandbox. This is where you can test out pens to see which ones bleed through, try out new drawing techniques, or experiment with stickers and washi tape. Think of these pages as your journal's backstage, where all the preparation happens away from the main performance. It's a practical approach to reducing the fear of ruining your journal and a great way to discover what works best for you.

Creative Cover-Ups

So, you've made a mistake, and it's staring back at you, challenging you to fix it. Here's where you get to be creative. Mistakes are just opportunities in disguise. A smudge can become the shadow in a drawing, a misspelled word can be covered with a sticker, and an unwanted paragraph becomes the perfect spot to try out that new washi tape. Or, turn that mistake into a piece of art. Draw around it, write a reflective note on embracing flaws, or simply put a big, bold "Oops" over it and smile. Your journal is a reflection of life, and life is all about making it work, one way or another.

This chapter is not just about making peace with imperfection; it's about celebrating it. In your journal, every smudge, every crossed-out word, and every oddly shaped drawing adds character, tells a story, and marks progress. It's a testament to your journey, with all its ups and downs, captured on the pages of your journal, imperfections included. Remember, the beauty of journaling lies not in creating a flawless record but in authentically documenting your experiences, thoughts, and growth. So let those pages fill with the messy, beautiful reality of life, and watch as your journal transforms into a treasure trove of memories, lessons, and reflections, imperfectly perfect in every way.

6.2 Finding Time to Journal Regularly

In the whirlwind of daily life, where each tick of the clock ushers us from one task to the next, carving out moments for journaling can feel like trying to hold water in our hands. Yet, it's these moments of pause and reflection that can transform our day from a series of events into a meaningful narrative. Let's explore how we can weave journaling into the fabric of our everyday lives, making it as natural as our morning cup of coffee or evening unwind.

Integrating Journaling into Daily Routines

The secret to consistent journaling lies not in monumental shifts but in the subtle weaving of it into the rhythms we already dance to. Identifying pockets of time within our existing routines creates a seamless integration, making journaling an effortless addition to our day. Consider:

- **Morning musings**: While your coffee brews or as you sit down with your breakfast, take a few moments to jot down what you're looking forward to or your intentions for the day.
- **Lunchtime lines**: Use a part of your lunch break to reflect. A quick note about an interesting interaction or a thought that's been playing on your mind.
- **Evening reflections**: Before you turn in for the night, reflect on the day. What surprised you? What are you grateful for? This can be a soothing ritual that helps transition you into rest.

By anchoring journaling to habits already in place, it becomes less of an extra task and more a part of our daily essence.

Journaling on the Go

Life doesn't always allow for leisurely moments with our journal at a desk. This is where the concept of a portable journal comes into play. A small, easily carried notebook invites spontaneity, allowing us to capture life as it happens, whether it's during a commute, in a waiting room, or under a tree in the park. The benefits are manifold:

- **Capture the moment**: Thoughts and observations are freshest in the moment. A portable journal allows you to capture these with vivid immediacy.
- **Maximize unused moments**: Turn what would be idle time into productive reflection or creativity.
- **Inspiration everywhere**: The world outside your door is brimming with inspiration; a portable journal ensures you're always ready to catch it.

Setting Attainable Goals

When it comes to journaling, the adage 'less is more' holds true, especially at the start. Setting grandiose goals can lead to a sense of failure, which might deter you from journaling altogether. Instead, aim for consistency over volume. Start with manageable goals:

- **A line a day**: Commit to writing just one line each day. It's a small, achievable goal that can lead to a rewarding habit.
- **Timed journaling**: Set a timer for five minutes of journaling. Often, the hardest part is starting; once the timer is going, you might find it hard to stop.
- **Weekly themes**: Each week, pick a theme to explore in your journal. This provides direction without the pressure of daily entries.

Remember, the goal is to build a sustainable practice, not to fill notebooks at breakneck speed.

Prioritizing Journaling

In a world that clamors for our attention, prioritizing journaling requires intentional effort. It's about recognizing the value it brings to our lives and making space for it amidst our priorities. Here's how you can elevate journaling on your list:

- **Reminders and alarms**: Just as you might set a reminder for a meeting or to take medication, do the same for your journaling time. It's an appointment with yourself that deserves to be honored.
- **Visible cues**: Keep your journal in a place where you'll see it often. Out of sight is out of mind, but a journal on your nightstand or kitchen table invites engagement.
- **Communicate its importance**: If you live with others, let them know that your journaling time is important to you. This not only secures you the space to journal but also affirms its value in your life.

As you fold journaling into the fabric of your daily life, remember that its purpose is to serve you, to be a vessel for expression, reflection, and growth. It's not about adhering rigidly to a schedule or meeting a quota of pages. It's about creating a space where you can pause, breathe, and connect with yourself amidst the bustle of life. Whether it's a few scribbled sentences on a busy day or pages of reflection on a quiet evening, each entry is a step on your journey, a moment of life captured in words.

6.3 Dealing with Journaling Blocks

Staring at a blank page can feel like looking into a void where your thoughts should be. It's not uncommon to hit a wall, where words evade you, and inspiration seems like a distant friend. When the well of creativity runs dry, and you find yourself grappling with what I like to call 'journaling blocks,' here are a few strategies to gently nudge your muse back into the conversation.

Prompt Diversification

Keeping a diverse array of prompts at your disposal is akin to having a keyring full of keys, each ready to unlock a different door in your mind. Consider assembling a collection of prompts to cater to various moods and moments:

- **Emotion-based prompts**: "What made me smile today?" or "What's weighing on my heart?"
- **Sensory prompts**: "Describe today using only sounds" or "What scent brings back memories?"
- **Imaginative prompts**: "If I could walk into any painting, which would it be?" or "A day in the life of my coffee mug."

Having this eclectic mix ensures that you have access to a prompt that resonates, regardless of the mental or emotional state you find yourself in.

Switching Mediums

When words feel like stubborn locks refusing to yield, it might be time to pick a different set of tools. Switching your medium of expression can breathe new life into your journaling practice:

- **Drawing or painting**: Let colors and shapes do the talking. Even simple doodles can convey emotions and ideas that words sometimes can't.
- **Digital journaling**: A change of scenery from paper to screen offers new tools and formats for expression, such as typing, digital art, or even audio entries.
- **Collage**: Combining images, textures, and ephemera can spark new ideas and narratives, turning the page into a visual feast that tells a story all its own.

This shift not only circumvents the block but also adds layers and richness to your journaling, making each entry a discovery.

Freewriting

Consider freewriting your journal's version of a magic wand – a swift, powerful motion that clears the cobwebs and reveals hidden treasures. Set a timer for a few minutes and write non-stop. The rules are simple:

- Don't worry about grammar, spelling, or making sense.
- Let go of the need for a beginning, middle, and end.
- Write whatever comes to mind, no matter how disjointed or trivial it seems.

This process liberates your thoughts from the inner critic's grasp, allowing them to flow freely and uncensored onto the page. It's not about crafting a coherent entry but about unlocking the floodgates of your thoughts and emotions.

Seeking Inspiration

Sometimes, the spark we need exists outside the confines of our current environment or mindset. Venturing out, either physically or mentally, can reignite the creative flame:

- **New experiences**: A walk in a new neighborhood, trying a different cuisine, or even a conversation with a stranger can offer fresh perspectives and material for your journal.
- **Engaging with art**: Whether it's a visit to a gallery, listening to a new album, or watching an indie film, immersing yourself in someone else's creativity can stimulate your own.

- **Spending time in nature**: Nature has a way of soothing the soul and inspiring the mind. Observing the intricate dance of leaves in the wind or the serene flow of a stream can awaken a sense of wonder and curiosity.

By opening yourself up to new stimuli, you invite inspiration to come flooding back, often bringing with it a deluge of thoughts and ideas begging to be journaled.

In navigating the occasional blocks and dry spells that are part and parcel of the journaling journey, remember that creativity is not a finite resource but a well that can be replenished from many sources. Whether it's by mixing up prompts, changing your medium, unleashing the raw energy of freewriting, or seeking new experiences and inspirations, there's always a way to coax your muse out of hiding. The key is to remain open, curious, and forgiving of oneself. After all, every page – whether filled with words, sketches, or the imprints of a day lived – is a step forward in the continuous journey of self-expression and discovery.

6.4 Overcoming Self-Criticism in Artistic Expression

In the realm of your journal pages, where thoughts and creativity flow like a river, a dam called self-criticism often obstructs the stream. It whispers doubts, compares your splashes of expression to the oceans created by others, and sometimes, it might even convince you to close your journal for good. But here's a secret: that dam isn't as solid as it seems. It's made of mist, and with the right approach, you can walk right through it. Let's explore how to do just that.

Fostering a Growth Mindset

Imagine looking at your journal entries, not as final pieces set in stone but as steps on a path of continuous learning. This shift in perspective is at the heart of adopting a growth mindset. Every word written, every line drawn, is a brushstroke in your development as a journal keeper and as an individual. It's crucial to see each entry as a building block, adding to your skills and understanding. Here's how to nurture this mindset:

- **Celebrate progress**: Even if it's just noticing you're more comfortable holding a pen or finding one more descriptor for your emotions, it's progress.
- **Embrace challenges**: When a page doesn't turn out as planned, view it as a puzzle. What can it teach you? Maybe it's showing you a new style or a different approach you hadn't considered.
- **Reflect on learning**: At the end of each journaling session, take a moment to note what you've learned, not just about the subject you're writing or drawing but about the process itself.

Comparisons are Counterproductive

Scrolling through social media, it's easy to stumble upon journal pages that seem like masterpieces, each one more dazzling than the last. It's natural to compare your work to these highlights, but remember, social media is a gallery of best moments. Behind each of those posts are dozens of crumpled papers, erased lines, and the same doubts you might be feeling. Instead of comparing, focus on your journey:

- **Limit exposure**: If social media dampens your spirits, take a break. Your creativity needs space to breathe, away from the pressure of comparison.
- **Track your journey**: Keep a log of your journaling milestones. Looking back will show you just how far you've come.
- **Seek inspiration, not replication**: Let the work of others inspire you to try new techniques or explore different themes, but always through your lens.

Celebrating All Attempts

Your journal is a testament to your willingness to show up for yourself. It's a brave space where effort deserves celebration, irrespective of the outcome. To foster this environment of positive reinforcement, consider dedicating a section of your journal to celebrating all attempts:

- **Badge of effort**: For every entry that felt like a struggle, give yourself a 'badge' – a sticker, a star, or a simple checkmark. It's a visual reminder of your resilience.
- **Mistake of the month**: Once a month, choose a mistake and highlight it. Next to it, write what this mistake taught you or how it helped you grow.
- **Gallery of experiments**: Reserve pages for experiments with new styles or mediums. This gallery isn't about success; it's about exploration and the joy of trying.

Sharing and Support

One of the most powerful antidotes to self-criticism is sharing your work. It can be terrifying, yes, but it's also incredibly liberating. Finding a community or even just one person you trust can transform the way you view your journaling practice. Here are a few steps to start sharing safely:

- **Choose wisely**: Share with those who understand the value of constructive feedback and who support your growth.
- **Set boundaries**: Be clear about the kind of feedback you're looking for. If you're not ready for critique, it's okay to say so.

- **Celebrate together**: Make sharing a two-way street. Celebrate the efforts and progress of others, and let their journeys inspire you.

By stepping through the mist of self-criticism with a growth mindset, focusing on your path without falling into the trap of comparison, celebrating every attempt, and embracing the support of a community, you'll find that your journal becomes not just a book of pages but a vibrant, living testament to your journey. Each entry, with its imperfections and trials, becomes a stepping stone in your continuous path of growth and discovery. Here, in the safety of your journal, let your creativity flow freely, knowing that it's not just about the art you create but the person you become in the process.

6.5 Journaling During Emotional Times

Navigating through the stormy seas of our emotions can sometimes feel like an insurmountable task. Yet, it's during these turbulent times that journaling can serve as a lighthouse, guiding us back to shore. Let's peel back the layers on how journaling during emotional highs and lows not only provides a therapeutic outlet but also fosters deeper self-awareness and healing.

Embracing the Cathartic Process

When emotions run high, our initial instinct might be to bottle them up. However, allowing ourselves the freedom to express these feelings on paper can be incredibly liberating. Think of your journal as a trusted confidant, ready to listen without judgment. The act of transferring your emotions from mind to paper can provide a sense of release, transforming abstract feelings into tangible words. This catharsis not only lightens the emotional load but also offers clarity, turning jumbled thoughts into understandable sentences.

- Write without censoring yourself. Let the words flow, acknowledging every emotion without critique.
- Visualize each word as a release, a letting go of the emotion it represents.

Guided Emotional Entries

Sometimes, the intensity of our feelings can make starting the first line daunting. Here are some structured exercises designed to guide you through journaling during emotional times:

- **Writing letters that won't be sent**: Pen a letter to someone who has caused you pain or joy. Express everything you wish you could say. The act of writing without the intention of sending offers a safe space to truly be open.
- **Listing things for which you are grateful**: In moments of sadness or frustration, listing aspects of your life you're thankful for can shift your focus, bringing to light the positive amidst the storm.

- **Describing your emotions as weather patterns**: This creative exercise allows you to externalize your feelings, making them easier to understand and process. Is your anger a thunderstorm? Is your sadness a gentle rain?

These exercises not only provide a starting point but also encourage exploration and understanding of your emotions in a structured yet open-ended way.

Taking Breaks

It's important to recognize when journaling about your emotions starts to feel overwhelming. It's perfectly okay to step back and take a breather. Remember, this practice is meant to serve you, not become another source of stress. Honor your feelings and give yourself permission to pause. Sometimes, a little distance can provide a new perspective, and you may return to your journal with fresh eyes and a lighter heart.

- Set your journal aside and engage in an activity that brings you peace, whether it's a walk, a cup of tea, or a favorite song.
- Know that your journal will be there when you're ready to return, no rush, no pressure.

Seeking Professional Support

While journaling is a powerful tool for navigating our emotional landscapes, there are times when professional support is necessary. If you find your emotions are consistently overwhelming or if you're struggling to cope, reaching out for help is a sign of strength, not weakness. Remember, journaling is just one piece of the puzzle in managing our emotional health.

- Consider sharing your journaling insights with a therapist. Often, the patterns and thoughts we uncover can provide valuable starting points for conversation.
- Know that seeking help is a brave step towards healing and growth.

In folding journaling into our emotional toolkit, we find not only a method for processing and understanding our feelings but also a practice that enriches our journey towards self-awareness and emotional resilience. Through the highs and lows, your journal stands as a testament to your strength, a reminder of your growth, and a sanctuary for your heart and mind.

6.6 Managing Multiple Journals

Navigating through the world of journaling often leads to the accumulation of not just thoughts and reflections but also, quite literally, a collection of journals. Each one could hold a fragment of your world – a diary for daily musings, a sketchbook for fleeting moments of inspiration, a gratitude journal for moments of appreciation, and perhaps even a dream log. The beauty of having multiple journals lies in the freedom to explore different facets of your life and creativity. However, without a clear strategy, this freedom can quickly turn into chaos, with thoughts scattered across pages like leaves in the wind. Let's explore how to harmonize the chorus of your journals into a symphony of self-expression and discovery.

Purposeful Journaling

To prevent your journals from overlapping in content and purpose, a bit of intentionality goes a long way. Assigning a distinct role to each journal helps maintain clarity and focus. Imagine each journal as a vessel dedicated to exploring a specific realm:

- A **daily reflections journal** could serve as a space for introspection and the events of the day.
- A **creative ideas journal** becomes a haven for brainstorming and capturing sparks of inspiration.
- A **gratitude journal** offers a place to recount and cherish the positive moments and blessings.

This delineation ensures that each journal remains a dedicated domain, making your journaling practice more organized and purposeful.

Rotational Journaling

Incorporating multiple journals into your routine without feeling overwhelmed is akin to a dance – it requires rhythm and timing. A rotational approach allows each journal to have its moment in the spotlight:

- Dedicate specific **days of the week** to different journals. For instance, Sundays could be for reflection, Wednesdays for creative ideas, and Fridays for expressing gratitude.
- Alternatively, devote **weeks or months** to a particular journal, immersing yourself in a theme or practice before rotating to the next.

This method ensures that each journal receives attention and keeps your practice fresh and engaging.

Summarization Pages

To weave a thread of continuity through your collection of journals, summarization pages act as anchors. They provide a snapshot of your thoughts, ideas, and reflections, serving as a guide to the themes and patterns that emerge over time:

- At the **start of each journal**, dedicate a page to summarize its purpose and the kind of entries it will hold.
- **Update this page** periodically with brief notes on significant entries, insights gained, or recurring themes.

This practice not only helps you navigate your journals with ease but also offers a bird's-eye view of your journey, highlighting growth and shifts in perspective.

Digital Indexing

For those who are comfortable navigating the digital realm, creating a digital index or utilizing journaling apps offers a bridge between the tactile world of paper journals and the convenience of technology. This approach provides a centralized location to track themes, entries, and insights across all your journals:

- **Digital indexes** can be as simple as a spreadsheet with columns for dates, journal types, entry titles, and key themes or insights. This allows for quick searches and cross-referencing.

- **Journaling apps** often come with built-in features for tagging and organizing entries. By digitizing your handwritten pages or summarizing them in the app, you can merge the benefits of hand-written reflection with digital convenience.

Embracing digital tools for indexing amplifies the accessibility and utility of your journaling practice, ensuring that no insight is lost in the shuffle and that every reflection is a click or a tap away.

In threading together the diverse tapestry of your journaling practice – from carving out clear purposes for each journal and dancing through a rotational routine, to anchoring your insights on summarization pages and weaving in the efficiency of digital indexing – you create a structured yet flexible framework that supports your journey. This framework not only enhances the organization and depth of your reflections but also enriches the dialogue between the varied aspects of your life and creativity captured on the pages of your journals. Through this harmonized practice, each journal becomes a chapter in the ongoing narrative of your self-exploration and growth, with the seamless interplay between them painting a comprehensive portrait of your journey.

6.7 Dealing with Distractions and Staying Focused

In the whirl of our daily lives, where every beep and flicker demands our attention, carving out a quiet corner for journaling can feel like setting up a camp in the middle of a bustling market. Yet, it's precisely within these moments, amidst chaos, that journaling can anchor us, offering a haven of tranquility and a space for undisturbed reflection. Here's how you can build that camp, turning your journaling time into an oasis of focus.

Crafting a Journaling Ritual

Imagine a ritual as a series of deliberate steps, each one bringing you closer to a state of readiness and focus. This isn't about elaborate ceremonies but about simple, repeatable actions that signal to your brain: "It's time to journal." Consider these steps:

- Choose a specific **spot** for journaling. This could be a corner of your room, a favorite chair, or even a spot at your local café. The key is consistency.

- Set a **specific time** for journaling. Align this with when you feel most reflective—be it dawn, dusk, or the quiet moments in between.
- Have a **small action** that marks the beginning of your journaling time. This could be brewing a cup of tea, lighting a candle, or playing a particular song—something that, over time, becomes a Pavlovian call to introspection.

Quieting the Digital Buzz

Our digital devices, for all their utility, are wellsprings of distraction, especially when we're trying to journal. Here's a radical thought: turn them off. Not silent, not vibrate, but completely off. If turning off is not an option, try:

- Putting your phone or device in **another room**. Out of sight, out of mind holds true.
- Using apps that **block notifications** or restrict access to the most distracting apps and websites for a set period.
- Setting your phone to **"Do Not Disturb" mode**, allowing only critical calls to come through if necessary.

The Magic of Timed Focus

The Pomodoro Technique, a time management method developed by Francesco Cirillo, breaks work into intervals (traditionally 25 minutes), separated by short breaks. This technique can be a game-changer for journaling. Here's how:

- Set a timer for 25 minutes. During this time, your only task is to journal. No checking phones, no wandering thoughts.
- After the timer goes off, give yourself a 5-minute break. Stand up, stretch, take a walk—anything that feels like a small reward.
- Repeat the cycle. You'll find that not only does this help maintain focus, but the breaks also refresh your mind, making your journaling time more productive and enjoyable.

Centering with Mindfulness

Starting your journaling session with a mindfulness exercise can transform your approach, moving you from a state of distraction to one of deep focus. Before you begin, try:

- A minute of **deep breathing**. Close your eyes, inhale deeply through your nose, hold for a moment, and exhale slowly through your mouth. Repeat this several times until you feel your mind settle.
- A brief **meditation**. There are numerous apps and online guides for short meditations. Even just a few minutes can help clear your mind, readying it for the pages ahead.

- Practicing **grounding techniques**. This can be as simple as noticing and naming five things you can see, four you can touch, three you can hear, two you can smell, and one you can taste. This practice brings you fully into the present, the perfect place to start journaling.

By weaving these threads together—establishing a ritual, silencing the digital noise, embracing timed focus, and grounding yourself in mindfulness—you create a space where journaling moves from an item on your to-do list to a cherished oasis of reflection. In this space, distractions dissipate, leaving room for your thoughts to flow freely, unburdened by the chaos of the outside world. Here, in the quietude you've crafted, your journal becomes not just a repository of thoughts but a sanctuary for your mind, a place where focus flourishes, and distractions find no foothold.

6.8 Choosing the Right Materials

In the labyrinth of journaling, the tools you select—be they pens that glide effortlessly across the page or journals that beckon with their untouched pages—are not just instruments but companions on your creative voyage. Each mark they make, each page they fill, carries a piece of your story. Here, we explore the art of selecting these companions, ensuring they resonate with your spirit and amplify your voice.

Experimenting with Different Tools

Imagine standing before a buffet of journaling tools, where every flavor from fountain pens to felt tips, from leather-bound journals to digital tablets, is at your disposal. The invitation here is to indulge, to sample widely and without restraint. It's through this process of experimentation that the perfect alchemy of tool and creator is discovered. You might find solace in the weight of a traditional pen, or perhaps the boundless potential of a digital app unlocks new realms of creativity. The key is to remain open to the journey, allowing each tool to whisper its possibilities into your creative process.

- Try out various pens and pencils on different paper types to see how they interact.
- Explore art supplies beyond the conventional, perhaps watercolor or charcoal, and see how they feel in your journal.

Quality vs. Quantity

In the pursuit of the perfect journaling setup, it's easy to fall into the trap of accumulating an arsenal of supplies, seduced by the promise that more is better. Yet, often, it's a select few chosen with care that become the stalwarts of your practice. A single well-crafted notebook or a pen that fits just right in your hand can elevate the experience, transforming the act of journaling into a ritual imbued with personal significance. It's not the quantity of tools but the quality of experience they provide that enriches your journey. Let joy be your guide in selecting these tools, for the true value of journaling lies not in the materials but in the stories they help you tell.

- Invest in a journal that feels like a treat to open, one that invites you to write.
- Choose pens or art supplies that make the process enjoyable, even if it means having just a few.

Sustainability Considerations

As you draft the landscape of your thoughts onto paper, the shadow of environmental impact often looms large. In an age where sustainability is not just a choice but a responsibility, selecting eco-friendly journaling supplies becomes an extension of your values. Opt for journals made from recycled materials, pens that are refillable, and art supplies that tout environmental certifications. This mindful selection not only reduces your footprint but also adds a layer of intention to your practice, making each word, each sketch a testament to your commitment to the earth.

- Look for journals certified by environmental organizations.
- Choose refillable pens and pencils to reduce waste.

Organizing Supplies

A symphony of creativity often requires an orchestra of tools, and like any maestro, knowing where each instrument lies is crucial to the performance. Organizing your journaling supplies not only streamlines your practice but also transforms preparation into part of the creative ritual. Imagine a space where each pen, each notebook has its place, ready to be summoned at a moment's inspiration. This organization can be as simple as a dedicated drawer or as elaborate as a custom workspace, but the essence remains the same: a sanctuary where tools wait patiently for their call to action, ensuring that when inspiration strikes, you're ready to respond.

- Use containers, cups, or trays to keep pens and art supplies within easy reach.
- Consider a portable solution, like a pouch or case, for journaling on the go, ensuring your tools are always at hand.

In the realm of journaling, your tools are more than mere instruments; they are extensions of your voice, conduits for your creativity, and keepers of your thoughts. The act of selecting them—balancing experimentation with preference, quality with joy, sustainability with practice, and chaos with order—shapes not just the physical act of journaling but the very essence of the experience. In this carefully crafted space, every pen, every page holds the potential for discovery, inviting you to explore the depths of your imagination and the breadth of your spirit.

6.9 Keeping Your Journal Private

The pages of your journal are a sanctuary for your innermost thoughts, a space where the heart speaks freely, and the mind wanders without restraint. Here, in the quiet communion between pen and paper, privacy isn't just a preference; it's the very foundation that allows this unbridled self-expression to flourish. Recognizing the sanctity of this space is the first step in safeguarding it, ensuring that your journey within these pages remains untainted by the fear of prying eyes.

Understanding the Need for Privacy

Imagine your journal as a confidant, a companion that holds your joys, sorrows, fears, and dreams with unwavering loyalty. This relationship thrives on trust, the assurance that your revelations will remain within the confines of its pages. It's this trust that allows you to peel back the layers of your persona, exploring the depths of your psyche and the expanse of your imagination without reservation. Privacy, therefore, isn't just about keeping others out; it's about creating a realm where you can be utterly and beautifully yourself.

Physical Security Measures

In the physical world, our journals exist as tangible entities, vulnerable to accidental discovery or, worse, intentional intrusion. Taking practical steps to shield them can provide peace of mind, allowing your focus to remain on the act of journaling itself. Consider these measures:

- **A lockbox or safe**: Investing in a secure place to store your journal when not in use acts as a fortress, protecting not just the physical book but the sanctity of your thoughts.
- **Creative hiding spots**: Sometimes, the best defense is obscurity. Tucking your journal in an inconspicuous place, where only you would think to look, can be an effective deterrent against curious eyes.

Digital Privacy Tools

For those who have embraced the digital age, bringing their journaling practice into the realm of bits and bytes, privacy takes on a new dimension. Here, the threats are less about someone stumbling upon your journal and more about the ethereal risks of data breaches and hacking. Fortify your digital sanctuary with these tools:

- **Password protection**: Ensure your digital journaling app or document is secured with a strong, unique password that acts as the first line of defense against unauthorized access.
- **Encryption**: Many digital journaling platforms offer encryption as an added layer of security, scrambling your entries into a code that can only be deciphered with your key (password).
- **Secure backups**: Regularly back up your journal entries to a secure location, such as an encrypted external hard drive or a cloud service that prioritizes user privacy. This ensures that even if your device is compromised, your reflections remain safeguarded.

Setting Boundaries

Often, the greatest risk to our journal's privacy comes not from strangers but from those within our personal orbit. Setting clear boundaries with family, friends, and roommates is crucial in maintaining the sanctity of your journaling practice. This conversation doesn't have to be fraught with tension; rather, it's an opportunity to express the importance of this space to your well-being. Here's how you can approach it:

- **Open dialogue**: Share with your loved ones the significance of journaling in your life and why privacy is paramount to this process. Most will understand and respect your request without further ado.
- **Specific instructions**: Be clear about your expectations. Whether it's not touching the journal without permission or respecting a 'do not disturb' sign when you're journaling, clarity prevents misunderstandings.
- **Mutual respect**: Just as you value your privacy, extend the same courtesy to others' personal belongings and spaces. This mutual respect creates a harmonious environment where personal boundaries are understood and upheld.

In navigating the delicate balance between openness and privacy, remember that your journal is a garden where your inner life blossoms. It's a place of solace, exploration, and growth, deserving of protection so that it may continue to be a source of comfort and discovery. By implementing practical security measures, leveraging digital tools to shield your entries, and fostering an atmosphere of mutual respect with those around you, you ensure that this sacred space remains inviolate. Here, within the pages of your journal, you're free to roam the vast landscapes of your soul, guided by the reassuring light of privacy that allows your true self to shine forth unencumbered.

6.10 Rekindling Passion for Journaling

There comes a time in every journaler's path where the spark seems to dim, not out of loss of love for the craft, but perhaps from the familiarity of routine or the pressures of expectation. In these moments, finding your way back to the joy and curiosity that first led you to open a blank notebook and spill your thoughts can feel like rediscovering a forgotten melody. Let's explore how to tune back into that rhythm and breathe new life into your journaling practice.

Rediscovering Your Why

Reflecting on the initial pull towards journaling can act as a beacon, guiding you back when the path seems obscured. Was it a desire to capture fleeting thoughts, an avenue for untangling complex emotions, or perhaps a means to document the journey of personal growth? Reconnecting with these motivations can illuminate the value that journaling continues to hold in your life, serving as a reminder that the essence of journaling transcends the act itself—it's about connection, exploration, and the continuous unfolding of your narrative.

- Take a moment to write about your first journal entry—what prompted it, how it felt.
- List the ways journaling has enriched your life, noting even the subtle shifts in perspective or moments of clarity it has provided.

Exploring New Journaling Styles

Introducing novelty into your journaling routine can reawaken a sense of adventure, inviting you to view your journal as a playground of possibilities. Whether it's venturing into visual journaling with sketches and collages, experimenting with poetic forms, or adopting a stream-of-consciousness approach, each new style offers a fresh lens through which to view your thoughts and experiences. This exploration not only revitalizes your practice but also expands your toolkit of self-expression, revealing new dimensions of your creativity waiting to be tapped.

- Dedicate a week to experimenting with a journaling style you've never tried before, noting how the experience shifts your perspective.
- Incorporate mixed media, using photographs, ticket stubs, or fabric scraps to add a tactile dimension to your entries.

Joining Journaling Challenges or Groups

The journey of journaling, while deeply personal, need not be solitary. Engaging with a community through challenges or workshops can reignite your enthusiasm, offering both inspiration and camaraderie. These shared experiences remind us that journaling is a universal practice, each person's approach as unique as their fingerprint, yet bound by the common thread of seeking understanding and expression. Challenges can push you out of your comfort zone in a supportive environment, while workshops offer new techniques and perspectives to weave into your practice.

- Look for online journaling challenges or prompts that resonate with your interests or areas you wish to explore.
- Join a journaling group or workshop to connect with others, share experiences, and gather new ideas.

Taking a Break

Sometimes, the most effective way to renew your passion for journaling is to step away for a while. This pause can provide the distance needed to gain perspective, allowing you to miss and thus rediscover the value journaling holds in your life. During this break, engage in activities that nourish your creativity and well-being, trusting that when you return to your journal, you'll bring with you a renewed spirit and a wealth of new experiences to document.

- Set a defined period for your break, whether a few weeks or a month, giving yourself permission to not journal during this time.

- Engage in alternative creative outlets or hobbies that refresh your spirit and could later serve as inspiration for your journaling.

In navigating the ebbs and flows of your journaling practice, remember that each phase—whether filled with fervent scribbling or reflective pauses—contributes to the tapestry of your growth. The act of journaling, in all its forms, is a testament to the ever-evolving narrative of your life. It's a space where the mundane can be magical, the chaotic can find order, and the silent whispers of your inner world are given voice. As we close this chapter, let's carry forward the understanding that journaling, like life, is a journey marked by cycles of passion, reflection, and rediscovery. Each page turned is a step towards deeper self-awareness, each word penned a celebration of our continuous becoming.

In the next chapter, we'll venture further into the heart of our journaling practice, uncovering more ways to deepen our connection to this art form and to ourselves.

Chapter 7

Mindful Journaling: Transforming Thoughts into Power

Imagine standing in front of a mirror, the reflection staring back at you filled with a mix of anticipation and uncertainty. It's the start of a new day, and the air is thick with possibilities and what-ifs. Now, picture wrapping those possibilities in words of encouragement and self-belief, turning the reflection into one of undeniable strength and potential. This isn't just an exercise in positive thinking; it's about setting the tone for your day, your week, your life through the power of daily affirmations and positive self-talk within the sanctuary of your journal. It's about transforming the mirror's reflection not just for the moment, but for the journey ahead.

7.1 Cultivating Positive Narratives

We talk to ourselves more than we talk to anyone else, yet we often overlook the tone and content of these internal dialogues. Affirmations are like seeds; plant them through your journal, and watch the garden of your mind bloom with positivity. Begin by identifying phrases that resonate with your aspirations and challenges. Instead of broad statements like "I will be successful," hone in on what success looks like for you, making it tangible and actionable. For instance, "I am making progress in my writing every day" roots your affirmation in the present and acknowledges your effort and growth.

- **Morning whispers**: Start your day by writing down three affirmations related to your goals and how you want to feel. Whisper them to your reflection, infusing your day with intention and empowerment.

- **Affirmation jar:** Create a physical or digital affirmation jar in your journal. Whenever you achieve something or overcome a hurdle, add a related affirmation. On tougher days, draw one to remind yourself of your strength.

Incorporating Affirmations into Routine

Make your journal a haven for positivity by dedicating spaces for affirmations. This could mean starting each entry with an affirmation, or dedicating entire pages to them.

- **Affirmation pages:** Designate a section of your journal for affirmations only. Decorate it with colors, stickers, or anything that uplifts you. Whenever you need a boost, you know exactly where to turn.
- **Weekly affirmation themes:** Each week, focus on a specific theme or area of personal growth. Tailor your affirmations to support this focus, reinforcing the mindset you wish to cultivate.

Reflecting on Affirmation Impact

The true power of affirmations lies in their ability to reshape our beliefs and perceptions. Regular reflection amplifies this effect, making it a crucial step in your journaling routine. At the end of each week, take a moment to reflect on how the affirmations influenced your thoughts, feelings, and actions. Did certain affirmations resonate more deeply? Why? This reflection not only reinforces the positive messages but also guides you in refining and choosing affirmations that align closely with your journey.

- **Affirmation review:** At week's end, jot down any changes in your mindset or accomplishments that align with your affirmations. Connect the dots between what you've been focusing on and the shifts occurring in your life.

Customizing Affirmations

The most powerful affirmations are those that speak directly to your soul, echoing your deepest desires and addressing your innermost fears. Crafting personalized affirmations requires introspection and honesty, making your journal the perfect workshop for this creative process.

- When crafting your affirmations, think about what you need to hear the most. Is it encouragement to take risks? Reassurance in your value? Guidance during uncertainty? Your journal entries likely already hold clues and themes. Use them as a starting point.
- Keep your language present tense and positive. Instead of saying, "I don't want to feel stressed," try, "I am embracing calmness with every breath."

In embedding affirmations into your journaling routine, you're not just filling pages; you're scripting the narrative of your life. It's a narrative where challenges transform into opportunities, doubts into assurances, and dreams into plans. Through mindful journaling, you wield the pen that writes your path, guided by the affirmations that light the way. Here, in the sanctuary of your journal, you have the power to shape your reality, one positive affirmation at a time.

7.2 Journaling Through Anxiety

Anxiety often feels like a fog that descends without warning, blurring our thoughts and quickening our pulse. It's a universal yet deeply personal experience, with triggers as varied as the individuals who face them. Through journaling, we can map this fog, charting its origins and discovering pathways to clearer skies. It's akin to turning on a lighthouse amidst a stormy sea, guiding us back to the safety of our own resilience and understanding.

Understanding Anxiety Triggers

The first step in navigating anxiety with your journal is to become a detective in your own life. Each time anxiety visits, jot down the circumstance, however mundane it may seem. Was it a crowded room that felt too close for comfort, or perhaps a day packed with deadlines? Over time, patterns emerge—threads that weave through your encounters with anxiety, highlighting common triggers. This insight is invaluable, transforming abstract fears into concrete challenges that can be addressed and managed.

- Start each entry with a quick note about your overall mood or anxiety level for the day.
- When you feel anxious, detail the context and any thoughts or events that may have contributed.

Structured Anxiety Logs

To transform your journal into a powerful tool against anxiety, consider structured logging. This technique involves documenting not just the moments of anxiety but also the surrounding context, thoughts, and outcomes. Each entry becomes a snapshot, capturing:

- **The trigger**: What event, thought, or situation sparked the anxiety?
- **Physical sensations**: Did your heart race, or did you feel a knot in your stomach?
- **Thoughts**: What was going through your mind at the moment?
- **Responses**: How did you react? Did you breathe deeply, step away, or perhaps reach out to a friend?
- **Outcomes**: After the episode passed, how did you feel? What did you learn?

This structured approach not only aids in recognizing patterns but also in evaluating the effectiveness of different coping strategies.

Coping Strategy Lists

Inside the covers of your journal lies the perfect space to compile a personalized toolkit against anxiety. This list is a living document, evolving as you discover what brings you calm and clarity. It might include breathing exercises that slow the whirlwind of thoughts, a playlist of songs that ground you, or even a collection of motivational quotes that remind you of your strength. When anxiety looms, your journal offers a ready repository of strategies to navigate through the fog.

- Keep a dedicated section in your journal for coping strategies, making it easy to find when needed.
- Regularly update your list as you discover new techniques that help mitigate your anxiety.

Reflective Writing on Progress

Reflective writing offers a chance to celebrate victories, no matter their size. It's about acknowledging the journey, recognizing the strides you've made in managing anxiety. Perhaps you faced a situation that once would have left you spiraling but found it a bit easier to navigate this time. Or maybe you're starting to notice the early signs of anxiety and can intervene before the storm hits full force. These moments of progress, documented in your journal, serve as beacons of hope and milestones of your growth.

- After a particularly challenging day or a successful navigation through a trigger, take a moment to reflect in your journal. What was different this time? How did you feel before, during, and after?
- Celebrate the small victories. Did you try a new coping strategy that worked? Write it down and give yourself credit for trying something new.

In crafting these entries, your journal becomes more than a collection of pages; it's a companion on your journey through the landscape of anxiety. It's a place where fears can be faced with words, where the fog of uncertainty is pierced by the light of self-awareness and action. Through the act of journaling, you chart a course towards understanding and managing your anxiety, making each day a step towards clearer skies and calmer waters.

7.3 Reflective Journaling for Depression

When the world seems draped in a cloak of grey, and the weight of your own thoughts pulls you down into the depths of despair, know this: there is a beacon of light within you, waiting to pierce through that darkness. This light is your ability to express, to pour out onto paper the tangled web of emotions that depression weaves around your heart.

Safe Space for Emotional Expression

Your journal stands as a bastion of safety amidst the storm, a place where feelings of sadness or depression can be expressed without fear of judgment. Here, you can lay bare your soul, shedding the layers of pretense required by the world outside. This act of vulnerability is not a sign of weakness but one of immense strength. It's in this space that you allow yourself to confront your emotions, to acknowledge their existence, and to start understanding their roots.

- Start your entries by naming your feelings. Simply starting with, "Today, I feel..." can open the door to deeper exploration.
- Allow yourself to write freely, without concern for coherence or structure. The aim is to express, not to impress.

Identifying Thought Patterns

Amidst the fog that depression casts over your mind, journaling becomes your lighthouse, helping you identify the thought patterns and cognitive distortions that often accompany this ailment. By tracking your thoughts and emotions, you begin to notice patterns—perhaps a tendency towards all-or-nothing thinking, or a habit of overgeneralization. Recognizing these patterns is the first step towards cognitive restructuring, a process where you challenge and modify these harmful thought patterns.

- Create a two-column table in your journal. In one column, write down the negative thoughts that frequently cross your mind. In the adjacent column, challenge these thoughts with evidence from your experiences that contradicts them.

Gratitude Journaling

In the battle against depressive thoughts, gratitude journaling emerges as a powerful ally. It shifts your focus from what's lacking to what's abundant in your life, however small or insignificant it might seem. This practice doesn't negate your struggles but offers a counterbalance, reminding you of the light that exists even in the darkest times.

- Dedicate a portion of your journal to daily gratitude. Each night, write three things you're grateful for that day. They can be as simple as a warm cup of tea or the comfort of your bed.
- Periodically, look back on your gratitude entries. On days when the world seems devoid of color, these reminders of life's small joys can serve as beacons of hope.

Letter Writing for Emotional Release

Sometimes, depression entangles us in emotions that are complex and difficult to express. Writing unsent letters in your journal provides a conduit for these emotions, allowing you to articulate feelings towards yourself, loved ones, or situations that have contributed to your state of mind. These letters are not meant for anyone's eyes but your own. They serve as a release, a way to say what needs to be said without fear of repercussions.

- Write a letter to yourself, offering compassion and understanding for what you're going through. Address yourself as you would a dear friend in distress.
- If there are unresolved feelings towards someone in your life, write them a letter. Pour out everything you wish you could say. The act of writing can bring clarity and, often, a sense of closure.

In these pages, you create a space where the tangled threads of depression can be unraveled and examined, where the heavy cloak can be lifted, if only for a moment.

Your journal becomes a vessel for healing, a place where the fog clears, and you can see yourself—not as depression paints you, but as you truly are: resilient, capable, and deserving of light. Through the act of journaling, you reclaim your narrative from the clutches of depression, threading each word with the strength of your spirit and the depth of your resolve.

7.4   The Relationship Between Journaling and Sleep

Tossing and turning, counting sheep, replaying the day's events or tomorrow's tasks—sound familiar? It's the nightly ritual many of us endure, searching for the elusive embrace of sleep. But what if the secret to a peaceful slumber lay not in sheep but in sheets—sheets of paper in your journal, to be exact? Let's explore how the intimate act of journaling can become your nightly lullaby, guiding you gently into the arms of Morpheus.

Pre-Bedtime Unloading

Imagine your mind as a bustling market, each thought a vendor clamoring for attention. This cacophony can make slipping into the tranquility of sleep seem impossible. Here's where your journal steps in, transforming from a simple notebook into a vessel to offload the day's mental merchandise. Writing down worries, tasks for tomorrow, or even a quick recount of the day acts like closing up shop for the night, allowing your mind to transition from the chaos of the day to the calm needed for sleep.

- Spend 10 minutes before bed jotting down anything that's weighing on your mind. Think of it as clearing the mental stage for the night's restful performance.

- Include a small section for things you're looking forward to. This positive note ensures your last thoughts before sleep are uplifting.

Dream Journals

Dreams are the mind's way of sorting through the day's experiences, a nocturnal narrative that often fades with the morning light. Keeping a dream journal by your bedside invites you to capture these fleeting stories, offering insights into your subconscious. More than just a record, this practice can enhance dream recall and, over time, deepen your understanding of your inner world.

- Keep your journal and a pen within easy reach of your bed. The less you have to move to record your dream, the more vividly you'll remember it.

- Write down everything you can recall upon waking, even if it doesn't make sense. Dreams speak the language of symbols, and seemingly random details can hold significant meaning.

Sleep Pattern Tracking

In our quest for quality sleep, understanding our patterns is key. Integrating sleep tracking into your journaling routine provides a panoramic view of your sleep landscape, revealing the terrain's peaks and valleys. By noting down your bedtime, wake time, and any disturbances, you map out a pattern that might explain why some days you feel like conquering the world while others feel like slogging through mud.

- Create a simple chart in your journal for sleep tracking. Include columns for the time you went to bed, woke up, and any notes on disturbances or dreams.

- Pay attention to how different evening activities (screen time, exercise, caffeine consumption) affect your sleep quality. These insights can guide you towards better sleep hygiene practices.

Relaxation Techniques

Pairing journaling with relaxation techniques can amplify the sleep-inducing effects of both practices. Engaging in a calming activity before journaling primes your mind and body for rest, making the transition to sleep smoother and more natural. Consider these techniques as a prelude to your journaling:

- **Guided imagery**: Visualize a tranquil scene, a place where you feel completely at peace. Immerse yourself in this imagery, engaging all your senses to deepen the experience.

- **Progressive muscle relaxation**: Work through your body, tensing and then relaxing each muscle group. Start from your toes and move upwards, releasing tension with each breath.

- **Breathing exercises**: Simple breathing techniques, such as the 4-7-8 method (inhale for 4 seconds, hold for 7, exhale for 8), can significantly calm the mind and prepare you for journaling and, subsequently, for sleep.

Incorporating these practices into your nightly routine not only sets the stage for journaling but also for a deeper, more restorative sleep. It's a ritual that tells your body and mind, "The day is done, and it's time to rest."

Through journaling, we find a pathway to peaceful sleep, a nightly practice that clears the mind, unravels the subconscious, and maps our journey through the night. It's a testament to the power of putting pen to paper, transforming thoughts into a lullaby that gently guides us into dreamland.

7.5 Emotional Release Techniques

In the tapestry of our lives, emotions color each thread, weaving patterns of joy, sorrow, fear, and love. Sometimes, these emotions intertwine too tightly, knotting into clumps that weigh heavy on our hearts. It's here, in the gentle pages of our journals, that we find a sanctuary for unraveling these knots, allowing our feelings to flow freely, transforming the tangled threads into a masterpiece of self-expression and healing.

Writing as Emotional Release

Think of your journal as a dam; behind its covers, a reservoir of unspoken words and unshed tears awaits release. When emotions surge, let them flow onto the pages, uncensored and unjudged. This act of pouring out your heart is akin to opening the floodgates—relieving pressure, making space for new growth, and cleansing the waters of your inner landscape. It's in these moments of raw authenticity that healing begins.

- Before you start, take a deep breath. Center yourself and set the intention of letting go.
- Write non-stop for a set period. Don't mind the grammar or coherence—focus on the act of release.

Physical Sensations and Emotions

Our bodies are the first to know what our minds often struggle to acknowledge. A tightening chest, a fluttering stomach, or a clenched jaw—these are the silent whispers of our emotional state, narrating stories our words have yet to form. By tuning into these sensations and documenting them in your journal, you bridge the gap between body and mind, fostering a deeper understanding of your emotional responses and their physical expressions.

- Start by closing your eyes and scanning your body from head to toe. Note any sensation, however subtle.
- Describe these sensations in your journal, alongside the emotions they accompany. Explore the connection between what you feel physically and emotionally.

Symbolic Letting Go

Sometimes, the weight of our worries and fears becomes too much to carry, their presence a constant shadow darkening our days. Here, your journal offers a canvas for a symbolic release—a ritual of letting go that transforms intangible burdens into something you can physically discard. Writing down your fears and then destroying the page acts as a powerful metaphor for releasing these burdens, a tangible act of surrender and renewal.

- Write down your worries, fears, or anything you wish to release on a separate piece of paper.
- Once you've poured everything out, tear up the paper, burn it (safely), or bury it. As you do so, visualize yourself letting go of these burdens.

Using Art for Expression

Words, powerful as they are, sometimes fall short in capturing the depth of our emotions. This is where art journaling steps in, offering a palette of colors and shapes to express what words cannot. Through the strokes of a brush or the smear of pastel, emotions find their expression in a form that transcends language, speaking directly to the heart. Art journaling becomes not just a method of release, but a journey of self-discovery, unearthing feelings and thoughts previously hidden in the shadows.

- Choose colors that resonate with your current emotional state. Don't think too much about the 'right' colors—go with your instinct.
- Let your hand move freely across the page, creating shapes, lines, or images that emerge naturally. The goal is expression, not perfection.
- Reflect on the finished piece. What emotions does it evoke? What thoughts or memories surfaced during the process?

In weaving these techniques into the fabric of your journaling practice, you create a rich tapestry of self-expression and healing. Each page becomes a step in your journey towards emotional clarity and resilience, a testament to the transformative power of journaling. Through writing, physical awareness, symbolic acts of letting go, and the use of art, you unlock new pathways to understanding and expressing the complex landscape of your emotions. Each technique, a tool in your arsenal, empowers you to face your feelings with courage and grace, weaving the threads of your experiences into a masterpiece of personal growth and self-discovery.

7.6 Gratitude Journaling and Happiness

Diving into the heart of gratitude journaling opens up a realm where acknowledging the good in our lives, no matter how small, can pivot our entire perspective towards happiness. It's like flipping a switch in a dimly lit room, suddenly everything is awash with light, and what was once overlooked now stands out in vivid detail.

The Science of Gratitude

Recent studies have highlighted the undeniable link between gratitude and an increase in well-being. It's fascinating to see how a practice as simple as noting down things you're thankful for can lead to significant enhancements in happiness and mental health. This isn't just about feeling better in the moment; it's about reprogramming the brain to default to a state of appreciation and positivity over time.

- Every time you list something you're grateful for, you're essentially strengthening neural pathways that make positivity and satisfaction more accessible states of mind.

Daily Gratitude Lists

The beauty of gratitude journaling lies in its simplicity. Every day, take a moment to jot down three things you're thankful for. These can range from significant life events to the seemingly mundane—the warmth of the sun on your skin, a message from a friend, or even the comfort of your favorite chair.

- The act of writing these lists focuses your attention on the present, cultivating a mindful approach to life where you're more attuned to the everyday blessings.
- This practice also serves as an anchor on challenging days, providing a tangible reminder of the positive aspects of your life when everything else seems clouded by difficulties.

Reflecting on Past Entries

One of the most rewarding aspects of gratitude journaling is looking back on your past entries. It's like reading a love letter to your life, filled with moments and people that have brought you joy, comfort, and support. This reflection isn't just a stroll down memory lane; it's an active engagement with your past that reinforces a grateful mindset and fosters resilience against future challenges.

- Set aside time each month to read through your gratitude entries. You might be surprised at how rich your life is with blessings and how this realization can shift your outlook on current difficulties.

Gratitude Prompts

To deepen your gratitude practice and keep it fresh, incorporating prompts can be incredibly helpful. These prompts can guide you to uncover layers of thankfulness you might not have considered before, enriching your journaling experience and expanding your capacity for appreciation.

- **Unsung Heroes**: Write about someone in your life who quietly makes your days better. What small acts of kindness have they shown you? How do they make you feel seen and valued?

- **Personal Strengths**: Reflect on a strength or talent you possess. How has it shaped your life? In what ways are you grateful for this part of yourself?
- **Simple Pleasures**: Focus on a simple pleasure that brought you joy recently. Describe the sensation, the context, and why it was meaningful to you.
- **Overcoming Challenges**: Think back to a challenge you faced and overcame. How did this experience strengthen you? What support are you thankful for having during this time?

Gratitude journaling is more than an exercise; it's a transformative practice that reshapes your interaction with the world. It teaches you to see beyond the immediate, often overwhelming, circumstances, to the vast tapestry of beauty, kindness, and strength that constitutes your life. In doing so, it not only enhances your happiness but enriches your entire journey, making each step, each breath, a testament to the power of gratitude.

7.7 Addressing Burnout Through Journaling

Burnout sneaks up like a thief in the night, pilfering our energy, enthusiasm, and efficiency piece by piece until we're left feeling hollow and disconnected. It's the result of prolonged stress, often stemming from our work-life balance (or lack thereof), leaving us in a state of emotional, physical, and mental exhaustion. But fear not, for your journal holds the key to unlocking the shackles of burnout, guiding you gently back to a place of harmony and vitality.

Recognizing Signs of Burnout

Before we can tackle burnout, we must first learn to see it coming. Your journal can serve as an early warning system, a place where subtle changes in your mood, energy levels, and outlook on life begin to surface. Here's what you might notice:

- A growing sense of detachment or cynicism towards aspects of your life that once brought joy or satisfaction.
- Persistent feelings of exhaustion, where even after resting, you don't feel recharged.
- A nagging sense that your efforts are meaningless or unappreciated.

Make it a habit to note down how you feel each day, not just physically but emotionally and mentally too. Over time, you may begin to see patterns emerge, acting as early indicators of burnout.

Journaling for Work-Life Balance

In the dance of life, work and play should move in harmony, each step calibrated to the rhythm of your well-being. However, when work leads too forcefully, the dance becomes unbalanced, stepping on the toes of your personal life and leading to burnout. Your journal can help you choreograph a more balanced routine by:

- Mapping out your current work-life balance, or imbalance as the case may be. Be honest about how much of your time and energy is devoted to work versus personal activities.
- Identifying areas for change. Maybe you need to delegate more, set firmer boundaries, or carve out uninterrupted time for relaxation and hobbies.
- Creating an action plan to restore balance. Set specific, achievable goals for integrating more non-work-related activities into your life.

Creative Outlets for Stress

Stress is an inevitable part of life, but it's how we manage it that determines its impact on our well-being. Your journal can be much more than a repository for thoughts and reflections; it can be a playground for your creativity, offering a much-needed escape from the pressures of daily life. Consider these stress-relieving journaling exercises:

- **Doodle your stress away.** You don't need to be an artist to scribble, sketch, or doodle whatever comes to mind. The act itself can be incredibly soothing.
- **Write a letter from your future self.** Imagine you're a year ahead, and everything has worked out. What advice would your future self give you?
- **Compose a 'stress story'.** Personify your stress and write a short story where you outwit, outplay, or outrun it. This can be both amusing and cathartic.

Action Plans for Recovery

Finally, charting a course out of burnout requires more than just recognizing the signs and easing the symptoms; it requires a proactive, structured approach to recovery. Your journal can serve as the command center for this mission, enabling you to:

- Set clear, realistic goals for your recovery. These might include daily self-care practices, seeking professional help, or setting boundaries at work.
- Track your progress. Celebrate the small victories along the way, and reflect on the challenges you encounter.
- Seek support. Whether it's confiding in a trusted friend or joining a support group, use your journal to remind yourself that you're not alone in this journey and to keep track of the support systems you have in place.

As you navigate the path from burnout back to balance, let your journal light the way. With each entry, you're not just documenting your journey; you're actively participating in your recovery, using introspection, creativity, and planning as your guides. Through the pages of your journal, you'll find not just relief from the symptoms of burnout but a roadmap to a more balanced, fulfilling life.

7.8 Self-Discovery Prompts

Peering into the mirror of your soul through the lens of your journal can be both a daunting and exhilarating experience. By asking the right questions, you engage in a dialogue with your inner self that can reveal depths previously unexplored. These prompts are your keys to unlocking those hidden chambers where your true essence waits to be discovered and understood.

Exploring Personal Identity

In the quest for self-discovery, understanding who we are beneath the roles we play and the masks we wear is vital. Consider these prompts as starting points for this exploration:

- **Core Values**: What values do you hold dear? How do these shape your decisions and actions?
- **Passions and Interests**: What activities light a fire in your heart? How do these passions reflect who you are?
- **Unique Qualities**: What makes you, uniquely you? Reflect on traits that set you apart from others.
- **Shadows and Light**: What are aspects of yourself you're proud of, and what parts do you shy away from? Acknowledge both with compassion.

By delving into these questions, you embark on a journey of understanding your complex, multifaceted identity, appreciating both your strengths and vulnerabilities.

Life's Turning Points

Our lives are dotted with moments that steer us in unforeseen directions. Reflecting on these can offer insights into our resilience, adaptability, and the evolution of our beliefs and dreams.

- **Milestones**: Recall significant milestones in your life. How did they transform you?
- **Challenges Overcome**: Think about the hurdles you've leapt over. What strengths did you discover in yourself through these challenges?
- **Unexpected Joys**: Sometimes, happiness finds us in the most unexpected places. When have you stumbled upon joy, and how did it change your perspective?

These reflections not only piece together the narrative of your life but also highlight the growth that often passes unnoticed in the day-to-day.

Facing Inner Conflicts

Inner conflicts are the friction points where our beliefs, desires, and fears collide. Addressing these through journaling can lead to breakthroughs in personal growth and emotional healing.

- **Conflicting Desires**: When have you been torn between two desires or paths? How did you navigate this?
- **Beliefs vs. Reality**: Are there beliefs you hold that conflict with the reality of your experiences? Explore these discrepancies.
- **Fear vs. Desire**: Often, what we most desire is also what we fear. Delve into these emotions and their roots.

Engaging with these prompts encourages honest introspection, fostering a deeper understanding of the complexities within.

Envisioning the Future Self

Imagining who we want to become can be a powerful motivator for change. These exercises not only allow us to dream but also to plan actionable steps towards realizing those dreams.

- **Letter to Future Self**: Write a letter to yourself five years from now. What achievements, experiences, and growth do you hope to read about?
- **Ideal Day**: Describe your ideal day in the future, in vivid detail. What are you doing, and who are you with? What makes this day perfect?
- **Bridge Building**: Identify the gap between where you are now and where you want to be. What steps, however small, can you take today towards your future self?

This forward-looking lens not only fills you with hope but also empowers you with a sense of direction and purpose.

Through these prompts, journaling transforms from a mere act of writing to a tool of profound self-discovery and reflection. It's a way to converse with your deepest self, uncovering desires, confronting fears, and illuminating the path forward. As you engage with these prompts, you're not just filling pages; you're charting the course of your own evolution, one honest word at a time.

7.9 Setting Intentions and Goals

Imagine waking up each day with a compass in hand, its needle pointing steadfastly towards your true north. This compass isn't forged from metal and glass but from the intentions and goals you've laid out in the pages of your journal. Here, in this personal tome of aspirations, clarity and focus emerge, guiding your energy towards the outcomes you desire most deeply.

The Power of Intention Setting

Picture your intentions as seeds planted within the fertile soil of your journal. Each word of intention acts as a commitment, setting the stage for the actions and decisions that will bring these aspirations to life. When you articulate your intentions in writing, you create a contract with yourself, a reminder of the path you've chosen to walk. This process transforms abstract desires into concrete objectives, crystallizing your focus and directing your energy towards achievement.

- Begin each day or week by jotting down a key intention. What do you wish to bring into your life or focus on? This could be as specific as improving a skill or as broad as cultivating more joy.

SMART Goals in Journaling

To turn these intentions into reality, they must be transformed into goals— not just any goals, but SMART ones. The SMART framework breathes life into your aspirations, breaking them down into achievable milestones. Here's how to apply this methodology within the pages of your journal:

- **Specific**: Clearly define what you want to achieve. The more detailed, the better.
- **Measurable**: Establish concrete criteria for tracking progress. How will you know when you've achieved your goal?
- **Achievable**: Ensure your goal is attainable with the resources and time you have.
- **Relevant**: Your goal should align with your broader life ambitions and values.
- **Time-bound**: Set a deadline. A goal without a timeline is just a wish.

Documenting your goals with this framework turns your journal into a roadmap, charting the course from where you are to where you want to be.

Reflecting on Alignment with Values

In the quest to achieve our goals, it's vital that they not only challenge us but also resonate with our core values. This harmony between goals and values ensures that our achievements bring fulfillment, not just success. Use your journal as a sounding board, a space where you can explore and affirm this alignment.

- For each goal, write down the values it supports. Does pursuing this goal nurture your sense of creativity, independence, community, or perhaps learning?
- If a goal seems out of sync with your values, consider this a sign to pause and recalibrate. Your journal can help you navigate these moments, offering insights into adjustments that might bring harmony back into your pursuits.

Regular Reviews and Adjustments

The journey towards our goals is rarely linear. It's filled with detours, roadblocks, and sometimes, scenic routes that offer unexpected insights. Regularly reviewing and adjusting your goals in your journal ensures they remain dynamic, adapting to the changing landscapes of your life.

- Schedule monthly check-ins in your journal to review your progress. What milestones have you reached? Where have you encountered challenges, and what have you learned from them?
- Be open to recalibrating your goals based on these reflections. Perhaps a goal needs to be broken down into smaller, more manageable tasks, or maybe a new opportunity has shifted your priorities.

In this ever-evolving narrative of intention and achievement, your journal stands as a testament to your journey. It's not just a record of where you're going but a reflection of how you've grown along the way. Through intention setting, SMART goal structuring, value alignment, and regular review, your journal becomes more than a collection of pages; it transforms into a compass, guiding you towards your true north with clarity, purpose, and adaptability.

7.10 Coping Strategies and Journaling

In the tapestry of life, where threads of joy and sorrow are interwoven, each of us seeks methods to navigate the intricate patterns of our emotions. Within the bound pages of a journal, we find not just a repository for our thoughts but a toolkit for emotional resilience. Here, we can gather our personal collection of strategies, a bespoke arsenal against the ebb and flow of life's challenges.

Compiling Personal Coping Strategies

Imagine flipping through your journal and finding a section brimming with your unique coping strategies, each a beacon during times of distress. This collection is personal, a curated list of what truly resonates with your spirit. It could range from a brisk walk in the park, engaging in a hobby that absorbs your full attention, to the soothing ritual of brewing a cup of tea.

- Start by listing strategies you've tried before, noting the outcome. Did it bring relief, clarity, or perhaps a sense of calm?
- Experiment with new strategies you come across. Your journal is a safe space to explore and assess their impact.

Evaluating Coping Mechanisms

Each entry dedicated to a coping strategy becomes a page of reflection, where its effectiveness is pondered. This isn't about judgment but understanding; what works splendidly one day might falter the next. The context, your emotional state, and even the environment play roles in how a strategy unfolds its benefits.

- After employing a strategy, jot down a few notes on its effectiveness. Consider factors like timing, duration, and your initial emotional state.
- Look for patterns over time. Do certain strategies consistently offer solace, or are some situational?

Creative Coping Through Journaling

Beyond being a vessel for documenting strategies, your journal itself can be an innovative tool for coping. Visualization exercises invite you to paint mental pictures of tranquility and safety, offering an escape when reality becomes overwhelming. Affirmations penned down act as anchors, grounding you in your worth and capabilities. Symbolic drawing, where emotions are depicted through abstract shapes and colors, offers a release that words sometimes cannot capture.

- For visualization, dedicate pages to describe places or scenarios where you feel utterly at peace. Revisit these descriptions when you need a mental retreat.
- Create a section for affirmations that reinforce your resilience and ability to navigate challenges.
- Use a page for symbolic drawing after a stressful day, letting colors and forms express what you're feeling.

Sharing Coping Strategies

This journey of compiling and evaluating coping strategies need not be solitary. Sharing with a journaling group or online community introduces you to new perspectives and methods, broadening your toolkit. It also fosters a sense of connection, reminding you that you're not alone in your struggles. As you share, you also offer support to others, creating a cycle of mutual aid.

- If you find a strategy particularly helpful, consider sharing it in your community. Your insight could be the lifeline someone else was seeking.
- Engage in discussions about coping strategies, keeping an open mind to new ideas and sharing your experiences with tried methods.

In weaving these elements into the fabric of your journaling practice, you craft not just a diary but a companion for your journey through life's ups and downs. This chapter, then, is more than a collection of words; it's an invitation to see your journal as a living, breathing entity that offers comfort, guidance, and resilience. As we move forward, let's carry with us the understanding that our journals are mirrors reflecting our innermost selves, tools that enable us to face the world with a steadier heart and a clearer mind. Let this knowledge guide us as we step into the next chapter of our lives, equipped with the strategies and insights we've gathered along the way.

Chapter 8

Beautifying Your Journal: The Essential Guide to Layouts

Picture this: you're sitting down with a fresh cup of coffee, ready to spill your thoughts onto the blank canvas of your journal. But wait, before the pen even hits the page, there's a pause. How do you want this collection of inner musings to look? Not just the words, but the whole vibe of the page. It's not merely about what you say; it's about how you present it. Like setting the table for a meal, the layout sets the stage for your words, giving them room to breathe, dance, or stand in solemn reflection. This chapter is all about that setup - creating a space that invites both writer and eventual reader (even if that's just future you) to dive deep, linger, and enjoy.

8.1 Foundation of Visual Journaling

The foundation of any great journal page isn't the words or the decorations you add (though those are important too); it's the layout. Think of your favorite book or magazine. There's a reason you can't stop flipping through the pages. It's the way the text flows, the balance between words and white space, and how elements are arranged that catch your eye and keep it moving. That's your goal here. Visual journaling is about blending text with elements of design to make your pages not just readable but visually compelling.

- Start simple. Even a basic understanding of layout designs can transform your journal from a cluttered mess to a masterpiece of clarity and intention.
- Consider the purpose of your page. Is it a reflective piece, a to-do list, or a combination? Your layout should serve this purpose, making the content both easy to navigate and pleasing to the eye.

Grids and Templates

Grids and templates aren't just for designers. They're your secret weapon for creating a cohesive look and feel across your journal. A grid can be as simple as dividing your page into halves, thirds, or quarters, using lines (real or imagined) to guide where text and other elements go. Templates, on the other hand, are pre-designed layouts you create once and reuse, saving time and ensuring consistency.

- Try drawing a faint grid on your page with a pencil before you start writing. You'll be amazed at how this simple step can improve the organization and aesthetic of your entries.
- Create a few template designs for different types of entries (daily reflections, weekly planners, mood trackers). Not only does this give your journal a unified look, but it also makes setting up new entries a breeze.

Symmetry and Asymmetry

Playing with symmetry and asymmetry can add an unexpected twist to your pages. Symmetry brings balance and harmony, while asymmetry can create dynamic tension and interest. Both have their place in your journal, depending on the mood or message you want to convey.

- For a calming, reflective entry, try a symmetrical layout, mirroring the placement of text and decorations on both sides of the page.
- Feeling a bit more adventurous? Go for an asymmetrical layout, with elements intentionally off-center or unevenly distributed. It's a great way to add visual excitement and energy to your pages.

Minimalist vs. Maximalist

Ah, the age-old debate: to fill or not to fill? Minimalist designs lean towards simplicity and ample white space, letting the content take center stage. Maximalist designs, however, embrace the motto "more is more," filling the page with color, text, and embellishments. Both styles have their charms, and the best part is, you don't have to choose one over the other.

- Experiment with both styles. You might find that a minimalist layout works best for your daily reflections, giving them room to breathe, while a maximalist approach adds excitement to your travel logs or project plans.
- Remember, the key to both styles is intentionality. Every element on your page, whether it's a single word or a burst of colorful doodles, should serve a purpose and contribute to the overall feel of the entry.

In this chapter, we've only just scratched the surface of what's possible when you bring a bit of design thinking into your journaling practice. The layouts, grids, and styles we've covered are starting points, meant to inspire and guide you as you create a journal that's not only a joy to write in but a delight to look through. With these tools in hand, you're well on your way to creating a journal that reflects not just the depth of your thoughts but the breadth of your creativity. So go ahead, play with layouts, experiment with symmetry, and decide for yourself whether you're a minimalist, a maximalist, or a bit of both. Your journal is a reflection of you, and there's no limit to where your creativity can take it.

8.2 Incorporating Calligraphy and Hand Lettering

When you open your journal, you're not just faced with a blank page; you're greeted with a canvas awaiting your personal touch. Here, between these lines, your words don't just tell a story—they show it. That's where the magic of calligraphy and hand lettering comes in, transforming your entries from simple text to works of art, each letter a stroke of your personality.

The Art of Beautiful Writing

Calligraphy and hand lettering are more than just fancy writing. They are the dance of the pen on paper, where each movement is deliberate, imbuing your words with weight and beauty. This isn't about perfect handwriting; it's about expression. Through the curves of calligraphy and the boldness of lettering, your journal becomes a reflection of your inner aesthetic, a place where the visual harmony of words matches their meaning.

- Begin by letting go of the notion that your handwriting isn't "good enough." Beautiful writing comes in many forms, each with its unique charm and character.

Basic Techniques and Tools

Embarking on your calligraphy or lettering journey starts with understanding the basics. The foundation lies in knowing that different tools create different effects. A brush pen, with its flexible tip, offers thick and thin lines based on pressure, perfect for modern calligraphy. A fine liner, on the other hand, provides uniform thickness, lending itself well to hand lettering and faux calligraphy.

- Equip yourself with a variety of pens. Experiment to find which ones feel right in your hand and match the style you're aiming for.
- Use practice sheets. Grids and lined guides can help maintain letter proportions and spacing until you feel confident enough to freehand.

Practice Exercises

Much like learning an instrument, mastering calligraphy and lettering takes practice. Yet, this practice doesn't have to be tedious. Infuse it with creativity and purpose by integrating exercises directly into your journaling routine.

- Write out your favorite quotes, experimenting with different styles for each word. This not only hones your skills but also creates beautiful pages filled with inspiration.
- Alphabet practice can be a meditation in itself. Slowly draw each letter, focusing on the form and feeling the pen glide on the paper. This can be a calming prelude to your journaling session.

Creative Lettering Ideas

Now, let's sprinkle some creativity into your pages with these lettering ideas. They can serve as headers, accents, or even the main feature of your journal entries, turning each page into a visual delight.

- **Decorative Headers:** Start each journal entry with a hand-lettered header. Play with styles—perhaps a bold sans-serif for energetic days or flowing script for reflective entries.
- **Illustrated Quotes:** Pair your favorite quotes with simple illustrations. Letter the quote in a style that matches the mood of the words, then add small doodles or borders that complement the theme.
- **Themed Word Art:** Choose a word that encapsulates your entry or your mood for the day. Design this word with embellishments, shadows, or patterns, making it the centerpiece of your page.
- **Marginalia:** In the margins, add small lettered notes, keywords, or even tiny motivational phrases. These can act as annotations, adding another layer of meaning to your entries.

Through calligraphy and hand lettering, your journal transforms into a personal gallery, each page a testament to the beauty of words made visible. This journey of embellishing your entries is about more than aesthetics; it's a deeper engagement with your thoughts and feelings, a way to highlight what matters most. So grab your pens and let your words flow not just from the mind but from the heart, crafting a journal that's not only a joy to write in but a treasure to behold.

8.3 The Role of Color Psychology

Imagine your journal as a canvas, where each stroke of color adds depth, emotion, and atmosphere to the story you're weaving. This isn't just about making pages pretty; it's about using color psychology to amplify the impact of your words, to set a mood, and to transform your journal into a vivid reflection of your inner world. Essentially, colors are more than just visual elements; they're tools that can evoke specific emotions and set the tone for your journal entries.

Colors Convey Emotion

Dip your brush (or pen) into the palette of your emotions through color. Ever noticed how certain colors can instantly lift your spirits, calm your mind, or even trigger a sense of nostalgia? That's color psychology at play. For instance, blue can instill a sense of calm and serenity, making it perfect for reflective entries. On the flip side, a dash of red might add energy and passion to pages dedicated to goals and ambitions.

- When selecting colors for your entry, pause and consider the mood you wish to capture or the emotions you're exploring. Aligning colors with these emotions can deepen the journaling experience and offer new insights into your feelings.

Color Themes

Setting a color theme for your journal pages is like choosing the soundtrack for a movie scene—it sets the backdrop, enhances the mood, and ties everything together. Whether it's the vibrant hues of a summer day or the muted tones of a rainy afternoon, color themes can bring coherence and depth to your entries.

- For a week or a month, experiment with a consistent color theme. Notice how this theme influences your mood and the tone of your entries. Is there a certain sense of continuity or rhythm that emerges?

Color Coding

Beyond aesthetics, color can serve a practical purpose in your journal through color coding. It's a strategy that combines the beauty of colors with the functionality of organization. Color coding can help you quickly navigate your journal, highlight important sections, or categorize different types of entries.

- Use different colors to mark distinct categories like gratitude, daily reflections, or creative ideas. This not only makes your journal more visually appealing but also turns it into an efficient tool for tracking your personal growth and ideas.

Experimenting with Color

The real fun begins when you start mixing, blending, and layering colors. This experimentation is not just about creating visually appealing pages; it's a process of discovery, of seeing how different colors interact, contrast, or complement each other. Through this exploration, you can stumble upon unique color combinations that resonate with your personal style and enhance the visual storytelling of your journal.

- Try blending watercolors for a background wash that adds a subtle hint of mood without overwhelming the text.

- Layer colored pencils or markers to create depth and interest. Start with light colors and gradually add darker shades to build intensity and focus.

In weaving color psychology into your journaling practice, you're doing more than just filling pages with hues; you're crafting an emotionally resonant and visually compelling narrative. Colors become a language all their own, speaking directly to the heart and enhancing the journey of self-expression and exploration. So next time you open your journal, think of your colors not just as decoration but as an integral part of your storytelling toolkit, each shade a word, each combination a sentence in the vibrant story of your life.

8.4 Stencil Art in Journaling

Imagine peering into your journal and seeing pages that look like they leapt straight out of an art gallery. Now, what if I told you that achieving such an artistic feat doesn't require the skills of a seasoned artist, but merely the playful heart of a crafter? Welcome to the world of stencil art in journaling—a place where intricate designs and whimsical patterns become as easy to create as tracing your name.

Easy Artistic Elements

Stencil art is the secret ingredient for those of us whose hearts yearn to create, but whose hands haven't quite mastered the freehand finesse of a paintbrush. With a variety of stencils at your disposal, your journal pages can quickly transform from plain to extraordinary, no art degree required. Think of stencils as your artistic sidekick, ready to leap into action and bring a touch of sophistication or fun to your pages with minimal effort.

- Start with a simple leaf or geometric pattern to add a subtle but effective backdrop to your writing.
- For a more prominent feature, choose a stencil that matches the theme of your entry—be it a coffee cup for your morning musings or a constellation for a night of starry reflections.

Creating Custom Stencils

While store-bought stencils offer convenience, crafting your own stencils adds a deeply personal touch to your journal. This process allows you to tailor designs specifically to your interests, themes, or even to the contours of your journal pages.

- Use thick paper or thin plastic sheets to create your stencils. Trace your design onto the material and carefully cut it out with a craft knife. Always work on a cutting mat to protect your surfaces.
- Inspiration for your designs can come from anywhere—your favorite quote, a memorable skyline, or even the silhouette of a cherished pet.

Incorporating Stencils into Layouts

Stencils are not just for decoration; they can play an integral role in the structure and layout of your journal pages. By strategically placing stenciled elements, you can guide the reader's eye, emphasize certain sections, or create a flow that enhances your narrative.

- Use border stencils to frame your pages, instantly elevating the visual appeal of your entry.
- For focal points, a large, bold stencil in the center of the page can serve as an anchor for your text, around which your words can dance and weave.

Combining Stencils with Other Media

The true beauty of stencil art in journaling lies in its versatility and the endless possibilities it presents when combined with other media. This fusion not only elevates the texture and depth of your pages but also allows for a playful exploration of color and pattern.

- Pair stencils with watercolors for a soft, dreamy background. Apply a light wash of color over your page, then, once dry, use a contrasting color through your stencil for a pop of definition.
- Markers and ink pads offer precision and vibrancy, perfect for bringing your stenciled designs to life with bold hues. Layer different colors for an added dimension or use metallic markers for a touch of glamour.
- For those who revel in texture, combining stencils with modeling paste or gesso creates a raised effect that's not only visually striking but also inviting to the touch.

Through the simple act of incorporating stencil art, your journal transforms into a vibrant tapestry of colors, shapes, and textures—a visual feast that complements the depth of your written words. It's a reminder that artistry isn't confined to galleries or studios; it thrives in the pages of your journal, brought to life by your own hands and imagination. So, next time you sit down to journal, reach for a stencil and witness how these versatile tools can add a new dimension to your storytelling canvas.

8.5 Creating Themes for Your Journal

When you open your journal, each page is a new adventure, a blank slate that whispers of undiscovered stories and unexplored emotions. Crafting thematic journal pages isn't just about beautifying your entries; it's a deeply immersive process that intertwines your narrative with visual elements, creating a unified aesthetic experience that resonates on a personal level. This section will guide you through the enchanting process of theme creation, from the gentle sway of seasonal themes to the rich tapestry of personal interests and hobbies.

Unified Aesthetic Experience

Imagine your journal as a series of galleries, each page an exhibit that captures a specific theme, mood, or idea. This cohesion in design and content doesn't just elevate the visual appeal of your journal; it creates an immersive experience where words and visuals dance together in harmony. Achieving this unified aesthetic starts with a clear theme that guides your choice of colors, motifs, and layout.

- Begin by identifying the central idea or emotion for your entry. This theme becomes the guiding star for all subsequent choices, from the palette to the decorative elements.
- Think about how you can visually represent this theme. For instance, a theme centered around tranquility might feature cool blues, serene landscapes, and fluid, undulating lines.

Seasonal Themes

Aligning your journaling practice with the rhythms of nature offers a refreshing way to connect with the changing seasons. Seasonal themes are not just about embracing the aesthetic of each season but about reflecting the inherent mood and energy that they bring.

- Spring might inspire themes of renewal and growth, using vibrant greens, floral motifs, and symbols of new beginnings.
- Summer could evoke themes of adventure and warmth, with sun-drenched hues, tropical patterns, and imagery of sunsets and beaches.
- Autumn calls for themes of reflection and gratitude, incorporating warm earth tones, leaf patterns, and harvest symbols.
- Winter invites themes of introspection and coziness, featuring cool blues, whites, and imagery of snowflakes and cozy firesides.

Mood and Emotion Themes

Your journal is a safe space where emotions and moods are freely expressed and explored. Creating themes based on specific feelings allows you to dive deeper into your emotional landscape, using visual elements to complement and amplify your introspection.

- For an entry exploring joy, consider a theme that's bright and buoyant, with sunny yellows, playful patterns, and imagery of laughter and celebration.
- When journaling through sadness, a theme with muted blues, gentle waves, and imagery of rain could mirror the complexity and depth of your feelings.

Personal Interests and Hobbies

Incorporating themes around your hobbies and interests adds a layer of personalization to your journal that reflects your unique identity. This approach makes each page deeply resonant, celebrating your passions and curiosities.

- If you're an avid gardener, themes of growth, with botanical illustrations, earthy tones, and gardening tools, can make your entries bloom with life.
- For the wanderlust-filled soul, themes of travel and exploration, using maps, stamps, and vibrant snapshots of different cultures, can transform your journal into a world tour.

In weaving these thematic threads through the pages of your journal, you're not just creating a visually cohesive masterpiece; you're crafting a deeply personal narrative that resonates with your journey, your emotions, and your passions. Each theme is a window into your world, inviting anyone who flips through your journal—be it your future self or a loved one—into the rich, vibrant tapestry of your life. So, as you turn the page and ponder the theme of your next entry, remember that you're not just decorating a page; you're illuminating a story, one theme at a time.

8.6 The Art of Collage in Journal Entries

Diving into the world of collage breathes a new and vibrant life into the pages of your journal. This isn't just about sticking photos or magazine cutouts onto paper; it's about weaving a visual narrative that complements your written words, creating a rich tapestry that tells your story in colors, textures, and shapes. Collage allows for a dynamic exploration of themes, memories, and dreams, transforming your journal into a multidimensional canvas that captures the essence of your experiences and emotions.

Collage as Visual Storytelling

Imagine each collage piece as a character in your story. Photos, magazine clippings, ticket stubs, and ephemera, each holds a piece of a larger narrative waiting to be told. The beauty of collage as visual storytelling lies in its ability to layer these elements, creating depth and context that words alone may not fully capture. It's a dialogue between the tangible and the abstract, where a snippet of text from a magazine or the color palette of a photograph can evoke memories, feelings, or dreams.

- Start by selecting elements that resonate with the theme or emotion of your entry. Think about the story you want to tell and choose pieces that contribute to that narrative.
- Arrange your selected elements loosely on the page before gluing them down. This gives you the flexibility to adjust the layout until it feels just right.

Techniques and Composition

The secret to a visually appealing collage lies in mastering the balance between chaos and order. It's about knowing when to add more elements for richness and when to hold back for clarity. Here are some techniques and tips to guide you:

- Layering: Begin with larger pieces as your background and gradually add smaller details. This creates a sense of depth and dimension.
- Balancing elements: Pay attention to the distribution of colors, textures, and sizes across your page. Aim for a composition that feels harmonious yet dynamic.
- White space: Remember, empty space is a powerful element in itself. It offers a visual rest, preventing your collage from feeling cluttered.

Collage as Emotional Expression

Your journal is a sanctuary for your innermost thoughts and feelings, and collage offers a unique way to express those emotions visually. It allows for the exploration of complex feelings that might be difficult to articulate in words, providing a visual language for your emotional landscape. For example, a collage exploring the theme of loneliness might mix stark, empty landscapes with images of solitary figures or objects, using texture and color to convey a sense of isolation and longing.

- Reflect on the emotion you wish to express and select elements that evoke that feeling for you. Don't overthink it; trust your instincts and let the process be intuitive.
- Consider using mixed media, like paint or ink, to add another layer of emotional texture to your collage.

Incorporating Text

Text can add a powerful layer of meaning to your collages, creating a dialogue between the visual and the verbal. This can be achieved through handwritten notes, typed text, or cut-out letters and words from printed materials. The choice of font, size, and color of the text can significantly impact the mood and message of your collage.

- Handwritten notes add a personal touch, bringing your own handwriting into the visual narrative. Use these for reflective thoughts, quotes, or personal messages.
- Typed text offers a clean, uniform look that can contrast interestingly with the varied textures and elements of your collage. Consider using a typewriter for an added vintage feel.
- Cut-out letters and words introduce an element of playfulness and variety. Mix fonts and sizes for a dynamic effect or stick to a cohesive style for a more subtle approach.

Incorporating collage into your journal entries opens up a world of creative possibilities, allowing you to explore and express your thoughts, memories, and emotions in a visually engaging and deeply personal way. Through the thoughtful selection and arrangement of elements, the exploration of complex emotions, and the incorporation of text, your journal becomes a living, breathing work of art—a testament to the richness of your inner world and the beauty of your personal journey.

8.7 Using Nature Elements in Your Journal

The whisper of leaves, the rugged texture of bark, the softness of a flower petal - nature holds an endless array of sensations that beg to be captured. By inviting these elements into the pages of your journal, you not only create a tactile and visually rich experience but also forge a deeper connection with the world around you. This section explores how to seamlessly integrate nature's bounty into your journaling practice, turning each page into a celebration of the natural world.

Bringing the Outside In

Imagine your journal as a sanctuary where the outside world can flourish in harmony with your inner thoughts and reflections. Incorporating elements from nature such as pressed flowers, leaves, or even grains of sand and soil can transform your journal into a tangible record of your physical surroundings.

- Pressed flowers and leaves can serve as bookmarks or embellishments that add a burst of life and color to your pages. Remember to choose specimens that are not protected or endangered.
- A small pouch or envelope glued to a page can hold treasures like sand from a memorable beach visit or soil from a beloved hiking trail, creating a tactile memory that complements your written words.

Nature Prints and Rubbings

Nature offers an exquisite palette of textures and patterns, from the intricate veins of a leaf to the rough surface of tree bark. Capturing these details through prints and rubbings adds unique visual elements to your journal, each imprint a testament to the beauty of the natural world.

- For leaf rubbings, place a leaf under a page of your journal and gently rub the side of a crayon or pencil over the surface, revealing the delicate patterns of the veins.
- Ink prints of flowers or small objects can be made by lightly coating them with ink and pressing them onto your page, creating a stunning, one-of-a-kind impression.

Sustainability and Respect

As we draw inspiration from nature, it's crucial to do so with mindfulness and respect. Sustainability should be at the heart of our journaling practice, ensuring that our creative pursuits do not harm the environment or deplete its resources.

- Always collect natural materials responsibly. Take only fallen leaves, flowers, or other elements that won't harm the plant or its ecosystem.
- Consider the legality and ethics of collecting certain items, especially from protected areas. When in doubt, leave it and instead capture the moment with a sketch or photograph.

Nature as Inspiration

The natural world is not just a source of materials; it's a wellspring of inspiration that can influence every aspect of our journaling, from themes and layouts to color schemes. By observing and absorbing the subtle nuances of our surroundings, we can infuse our pages with the essence of the outdoors.

- Let the colors of the seasons guide your palette, from the fresh greens of spring to the rich golds and reds of autumn.
- Themes inspired by nature, such as growth, renewal, or change, can offer fresh perspectives and insights into our personal journeys.
- Sketching or photographing scenes from nature can provide reference material for future journal entries, allowing you to recreate the tranquility, beauty, or wildness of the outdoors on your pages.

In weaving nature into our journals, we create a bridge between the external world and our internal landscape, crafting pages that resonate with the beauty, complexity, and diversity of the environment. Through pressed botanicals, nature prints, sustainable practices, and inspired themes, our journals become living documents that celebrate our connection to the earth, inviting us to explore, reflect, and grow with each turn of the page.

8.8 Seasonal Decorations and Motifs

With each season's turn, the world creates a new cloak, offering a fresh palette of colors, textures, and themes for us to explore in our journaling. Embracing these seasonal changes not only diversifies the visual appeal of our pages but also aligns our creative expression with the natural rhythm of life. This section delves into how seasonal decorations and motifs can enrich our journals, turning them into vibrant chronicles of the year's passage.

- Crafting decorations that reflect the essence of each season can transform your journal into a dynamic canvas that mirrors the external world. Imagine delicate snowflake cutouts adorning your winter entries or vibrant leaf stamps heralding the arrival of fall.

- Drawing inspiration from seasonal flora and fauna not only adds a whimsical touch to your pages but also serves as a reminder of the transient beauty of nature. Sketch a cluster of spring blossoms or a winter bird to bring a piece of the season to life in your journal.

- Reflecting on seasonal traditions and celebrations through your journaling can deepen your connection to both the time of year and your personal or cultural heritage. Decorate a page with symbols of a harvest festival or write about the significance of the first snowfall, weaving your experiences with the broader tapestry of the season.

By integrating seasonal decorations and motifs into our journals, we create not just a record of our thoughts and experiences but a vibrant, ever-evolving artwork that reflects the beauty and diversity of the world around us. Each season brings its own story, its own mood, and its own colors, and by capturing these in our pages, we celebrate the cycle of life and the endless inspiration it provides.

The rhythm of the seasons not only influences the world around us but also the canvas of our journals. Each season whispers its own unique stories, painting our pages with its characteristic hues and themes. Here, we explore how to infuse your journaling practice with the spirit of each season, making your entries a reflection of the changing world outside your window.

Celebrating the Seasons

The cyclical nature of the seasons offers a rich backdrop for our journaling practice, inviting us to align our pages with the essence of the current time of year. This alignment not only enhances the aesthetic appeal of our journals but also deepens our connection to the natural world and its rhythms.

- For spring, you might incorporate motifs of renewal and rebirth, such as budding flowers or the vibrant greens of new foliage. These elements can serve as a metaphor for personal growth and new beginnings.

- Summer pages could burst with the energy and warmth of the season, using bright colors, sun motifs, and imagery of outdoor adventures to capture the essence of long, sun-filled days.

- As autumn rolls in, reflect the season's mood of transition and reflection with warm tones, falling leaves, and harvest themes. This can be a time for gratitude and taking stock of the year's bounty.

- Winter entries can embrace the quiet and introspection of the season, with cool colors, snowflakes, and cozy indoor scenes. It's a perfect time for introspective writing, planning, and setting intentions for the new year.

Handmade Elements

Adding handmade elements to your journal not only personalizes your entries but also adds a tactile dimension to your pages. These DIY decorations can vary from simple doodles and sketches to more elaborate crafts, depending on your time and inclination.

- Sketch or watercolor seasonal scenes directly onto your pages. A simple illustration of a leaf-strewn path in autumn or a snow-covered landscape in winter can instantly evoke the mood of the season.
- Craft small items like paper snowflakes, mini garlands, or pressed flower bookmarks. These can be tucked into your journal as removable decorations or glued in as permanent embellishments.
- Experiment with mixed media to create textured backgrounds that reflect the season. Layering paper, fabric scraps, and natural materials like pressed leaves can create a visually engaging and tactile experience.

Cultural and Personal Celebrations

Our journals are not just records of our daily lives; they're also archives of our cultural heritage and personal milestones. Incorporating decorations and motifs that reflect the cultural and personal significance of seasonal celebrations can add depth and meaning to our entries.

- Document holiday traditions with themed decorations, such as lanterns for Diwali, menorahs for Hanukkah, or pumpkins for Halloween. These symbols can serve as prompts for writing about the significance of these celebrations in your life.
- Mark personal milestones that align with the seasons, such as birthdays, anniversaries, or significant achievements. Decorate these entries with symbols that reflect both the season and the nature of the celebration, blending personal and universal themes.

Reflective Seasonal Entries

Each season, with its unique characteristics and mood, offers a lens through which we can view and reflect upon our lives. Creating reflective journal entries that explore our connection to the season can deepen our understanding of ourselves and our place in the natural cycle.

- Reflect on the transition between seasons and what it signifies for you personally. Are you inspired by the promise of spring, invigorated by the energy of summer, reflective in the face of autumn's changes, or introspective as winter descends?
- Consider how the current season affects your mood, activities, and outlook. Use seasonal motifs and decorations to underscore these reflections, making the connection between your inner world and the outer world visually apparent.

- Explore the themes and lessons each season brings. Spring might prompt thoughts on growth and renewal, summer on adventure and exploration, autumn on harvest and gratitude, and winter on rest and renewal. Decorate your pages with symbols and colors that resonate with these themes, creating a visual narrative that complements your written reflections.

By weaving the essence of the seasons into our journals, we create a living document that not only chronicles our journey through the year but also celebrates the beauty and diversity of the natural world. Through thoughtful decorations, handmade elements, and reflective writing, our journals become a testament to the cyclical nature of life, reminding us of the constant ebb and flow of time and the ever-present opportunity for growth and renewal. So as you turn the page to a new season, let your journal be a space where the outside world meets your inner landscape, creating a rich tapestry of memories, reflections, and aspirations that are as vibrant and varied as the seasons themselves.

8.9   Personalizing Your Journal Cover

The cover of your journal is the first thing you see before the magic of your thoughts spills onto the page. It sets the tone for your journaling experience, acting as a gateway to your inner world. Making this cover distinctly yours isn't just about aesthetics; it's about crafting a beacon that calls to you, inviting you into the world of words and creativity that lies within. This section explores ways to transform your journal cover into a personal emblem that resonates with your spirit and ignites your passion for journaling each time you see it.

First Impressions Matter

Consider your journal cover as the welcoming committee for your journaling practice. It's more than just a protective layer; it's the first impression, the initial handshake between you and your thoughts. Personalizing this cover means creating a visual and tactile reminder of what your journal represents to you, be it a sanctuary of peace, a garden of creativity, or a vault of memories. The process of personalizing your journal cover is a ritual in itself, marking the beginning of your journey with each new book.

- Reflect on what your ideal journal cover would convey. Does it whisper secrets of untold stories, or does it boldly proclaim your creative endeavors? Use this vision as your guiding star.

DIY Cover Ideas

The beauty of DIY projects lies in their ability to transform the ordinary into the extraordinary. With a few simple materials and a dash of creativity, your journal cover can become a masterpiece that reflects your unique style and preferences. Here are a few ideas to get you started:

- **Fabric Covers:** Wrapping your journal in a piece of fabric that speaks to you is not only visually appealing but also adds a tactile element to your journal. Choose a fabric that resonates with your personality, whether it's a serene floral print, a vibrant geometric pattern, or a soft, comforting texture.

- **Paint and Decoupage:** For those who love to play with colors, painting your journal cover is a way to make a bold statement. Alternatively, decoupage using cutouts from magazines, wrapping paper, or even old photographs can create a collage of inspiration on your cover.

- **Embroidery:** Adding embroidered elements to your journal cover introduces a personal touch that is both elegant and timeless. Simple designs like initials, favorite symbols, or small motifs add character and sophistication to your journal.

Inspirational Quotes and Art

Adorning your journal cover with quotes or artwork that inspire you turns it into a beacon of motivation. Every time you reach for your journal, these words or images serve as a reminder of your goals, dreams, and the values that guide your life.

- Choose a quote that acts as a mantra for your journaling practice. Hand-letter this quote on your cover or use stamps or stickers for a different effect.

- Personal artwork, whether it's a sketch, a painting, or a print, adds a layer of originality to your cover. This could be an abstract representation of your journaling journey, a symbol that holds personal significance, or simply an image that brings you joy.

Protection and Durability

While aesthetics are important, ensuring your journal cover is both protective and durable is crucial. After all, this journal is a companion on your life's journey, and it needs to withstand the adventures you'll embark on together.

- Consider materials that not only look good but also offer a layer of protection to the pages within. Leather or thick fabric covers, for instance, provide durability while adding an element of luxury.

- For those who prefer a more hands-on approach, applying a clear sealant over painted or decoupaged covers can protect your artwork from wear and tear, ensuring your journal remains beautiful for years to come.

In personalizing your journal cover, you're doing more than just decorating an object. You're creating a talisman that holds the essence of your journaling practice, a visual and tactile representation of your journey through words and creativity. This cover becomes a symbol of your commitment to exploration, reflection, and growth, inviting you into the world within its pages with each glance. So, take the time to craft a cover that speaks to your heart, for it is the first step into the boundless realms of imagination and introspection that await you.

8.10 Organizing Your Journal Aesthetically

Your journal, a personal haven for thoughts, dreams, and reflections, deserves a touch of order dressed in the beauty of design. The marriage of visual harmony and functionality not only elevates the journaling experience but also transforms your journal into a place of inspiration and serenity. Imagine flipping through pages where each section seamlessly flows into the next, where finding a cherished memory or a pivotal reflection is as simple as it is delightful.

Visual Harmony and Functionality

Striking a balance between aesthetics and usability turns your journal into an inviting space you're eager to return to day after day. Consider how the arrangement of elements on each page can enhance both the appearance and the practicality of your journal.

- Use color coding not just for its visual appeal but also to delineate sections, making navigation intuitive.
- Align your text and images in a way that guides the eye naturally across the page. Let there be a rhythm to how the content is presented, making each entry not only a joy to create but also to revisit.

Tabs and Dividers

Tabs and dividers are more than just organizational tools; they are opportunities to inject creativity and personal flair into your journal.

- Fabricate tabs from washi tape, colored paper, or even repurposed materials, adding a tactile element to your journal. Decorate each tab with symbols, tiny drawings, or hand-lettered labels reflecting the content of the sections they demarcate.
- Use dividers to separate themes, months, or types of entries. These can be full-page illustrations, collages, or simply beautifully designed quotes that introduce the next section, turning the act of sectioning your journal into an artistic endeavor.

Decorative Indexing

An index need not be a dry list of page numbers and titles. Transform it into a work of art that beckons you into the depths of your journal.

- Embellish your index with icons or doodles next to each entry, providing a visual cue of the content.
- Consider using different colors or fonts for various categories of entries, making the index not only a guide but a colorful overview of your journal's diversity.

Aesthetic Consistency

While creativity knows no bounds, a thread of consistency weaves through your journal, tying it together into a cohesive whole. This doesn't mean stifling your creativity but rather finding a style or theme that resonates with you and letting it echo throughout your pages.

- Choose a color palette that reflects your mood, the season, or the overall theme of your journal. Let these colors recur in subtle ways, whether in the headers, the page numbers, or the accents used in illustrations.

- Decide on a few key motifs or symbols that hold meaning for you and let them reappear across your journal. This could be as simple as a leaf design that pops up in corners or a specific set of stamps you use for date markings.

As we wrap up this exploration of organizing your journal with an eye for aesthetics, remember that your journal is a reflection of you. It's a canvas where your inner world spills out in words and visuals, where memories are preserved, and dreams are mapped. The harmony between beauty and function isn't just about creating a pleasing journal but about crafting a space that invites exploration, reflection, and creativity. As you continue on your journaling journey, let these principles guide you in creating a journal that isn't just organized, but a joy to fill and to flip through. Onward now, to the next chapter, where new insights and inspirations await to further enrich your journaling adventure.

Chapter 9

Merging Methods for a Masterpiece

Picture this: your journal as a cozy living room, where every piece of furniture, every painting on the wall, and every knick-knack on the shelf tells a part of your story. Just like a well-decorated room doesn't stick to just one style—modern here, a touch of vintage there, maybe some industrial chic for good measure—your journal doesn't have to be monogamous with its method. Mixing it up is where the magic happens. It's about creating a space that feels entirely you, eclectic yet harmonious. So, let's talk about how to blend different journaling methods to capture all the facets of your life, making your journal not just a book, but a home for your thoughts and creativity.

9.1 Synergy of Techniques

When bullet journaling meets art journaling, and they both bump into digital journaling at the party, you don't get chaos; you get a symphony. Each method brings its strengths to the table—structure, creativity, and convenience. Imagine capturing your daily to-dos with the precision of bullet journaling, reflecting on your emotions with the expressive freedom of art journaling, and then seamlessly integrating digital tools for those moments when the pen isn't mightier than the keyboard.

- **Morning Pages** with a twist: Start your day dumping thoughts digitally for efficiency. Later, pick a sentence that stands out and use it as a prompt for an art journaling session.
- **Gratitude Lists** can go from simple bullet points to elaborate art pages, illustrating each item on the list or creating a collage that represents your gratitude visually.

Case Studies and Examples

Think about Sarah, who loves the outdoors. She uses her digital journal to jot down notes and snap photos on her hikes. Back home, she brings her experiences to life in her bullet journal, planning future adventures with lists and maps, and in her art journal, painting scenes that left her breathless.

Or consider Alex, whose bullet journal is the command center for their life, but who also dedicates pages within for mental health check-ins, using colors and visuals to express feelings that words can't always capture.

- These real-life examples show that combining methods isn't just possible; it's transformative.

Balancing Forms

The trick isn't just in the mixing; it's in not letting one method drown out the others. It's like making a smoothie—you want to taste every fruit you've thrown in there, not just the banana because you put too much of it.

- Dedicate sections within your journal for different methods, or even blend them on the same page—bullet points on one side, a watercolor landscape on the other.
- Digital tools are great for on-the-go moments. Voice-to-text features can capture thoughts when you can't write them down, and digital photos can be printed and added to your journal later.

Personalized Journaling System

Now, it's your turn. Think about what you need from your journal. Is it organization, creativity, or maybe a bit of both? Here's a simple guide to creating a system that feels just right:

1. **Identify Your Needs**: What do you want to track, explore, or express in your journal?
2. **Pick Your Methods**: Choose the journaling styles that best meet those needs.
3. **Experiment**: Mix and match methods until you find the blend that feels like home.
4. **Evolve**: Your needs might change, and so might your preferred methods. Keep tweaking.

Remember, there's no one-size-fits-all when it comes to journaling. It's deeply personal, and what works for one person might not for another. The beauty of merging methods is that it gives you the flexibility to create a journaling practice as unique as you are. So, go ahead, mix it up. Your journal is a living, breathing document of your life. Let it reflect every color, every shade, and every texture of your journey.

9.2 The KonMari Method in Journaling

Imagine your journaling practice as a closet full of clothes. Some pieces spark joy every time you wear them, while others have been languishing in the back, untouched for years. Marie Kondo's KonMari Method invites us to declutter our spaces, keeping only those things that bring us joy. Now, let's apply this principle to journaling. It's about curating your practice to include only what enriches your life, making each journaling session a source of joy and intention.

Journaling with Intention

The heart of the KonMari Method lies in its focus on intentionality and joy. In journaling, this means steering your practice towards themes, methods, and reflections that genuinely resonate with you. It's about asking yourself, "Does writing about this bring me joy? Does this method make my heart sing?" If the answer is yes, you've found your journaling spark.

- Reflect on the past month of your journaling entries. Highlight the moments that felt especially fulfilling or joyful.
- Experiment with different journaling styles over a week. Note which ones bring you the most satisfaction and why.

Decluttering Your Journal

Just as you would sift through your wardrobe, take time to declutter your journaling practice. This might mean streamlining the methods you use, focusing your content, or even organizing your physical journaling space to make it more inviting and joy-inducing.

- Review your current journaling methods. Are there any that feel more like a chore than a joy? Consider letting them go.
- Organize your journaling space. A tidy, welcoming space can significantly enhance your practice. Keep your favorite pens, notebooks, and other accessories in places that inspire you to reach for them.

Joyful Journaling

Joyful journaling emerges when we focus on what genuinely matters to us. It's about channeling our energy into themes and practices that uplift and fulfill us. This could mean dedicating pages to gratitude, exploring creative prompts that excite you, or simply free-writing about your day in a way that feels liberating.

- Each week, dedicate a session to journaling about something that made you exceptionally happy. Use colors, stickers, or any other elements that enhance the joy of the experience.

- Create a "joy list" in your journal. Whenever you're unsure what to write about, pick an item from the list and explore it in your entry.

Reflecting on What Matters

In the whirlwind of daily life, it's easy to lose sight of our core values and goals. The KonMari Method in journaling encourages us to pause and reflect on what truly matters to us. This reflection can help realign our journaling practice with our deepest values, ensuring that it remains a source of joy and purpose.

- At the start of each month, jot down your key goals, values, and what you're grateful for. Use these as anchors for your journaling throughout the month.
- Consider creating a vision board within your journal. Fill it with images, quotes, and anything else that reflects your aspirations and values. Revisit and update it as you grow and evolve.

In applying the KonMari Method to journaling, we're not just tidying up our practices; we're crafting a space that resonates with joy, intention, and personal growth. It's about making each page, each entry, a testimony to the things that truly matter to us. By focusing on what brings us joy, we ensure our journaling practice remains a vibrant and fulfilling part of our journey.

9.3 Journaling for Career Development

In the tapestry of life, your career is one of the most intricate patterns you weave. It's a blend of ambition, skill, and sometimes, serendipity. But what if you could add another tool to your kit, one that not only tracks your progress but also propels you forward? Welcome to the realm where journaling meets career development—a space where reflections shape futures, and pages turn into steppingstones.

Professional Growth through Journaling

Imagine your journal as a garden. Each entry you plant is a seed of thought, watered by reflection, growing into insights that can nourish your professional life. This space becomes a sanctuary for setting career goals, a workshop for problem-solving, and a gallery of achievements.

- Set aside time each week to outline your professional aspirations. Be as detailed as possible—what do these goals look like, and what steps will lead you there?
- After challenging work situations or significant accomplishments, dedicate a page to dissect what happened. What lessons can you glean, and how can they inform your future actions?

Skill Assessment Logs

In this journey, your skills are your compass, guiding you through the professional landscape. Keeping a log of these abilities allows you to chart your growth, identify areas ripe for development, and celebrate the milestones you reach.

- Create a skill inventory. List down everything you bring to the table, no matter how big or small. Next to each, rate your current proficiency and note any ideas for improvement.

- Regularly revisit this log, updating it with new skills acquired or progress made. This ongoing record not only tracks growth but also boosts morale by visually representing your development over time.

Networking and Mentorship Notes

The paths we tread in our careers are seldom solitary journeys. Along the way, we encounter guides, allies, and fellow travelers. Documenting these interactions in your journal can turn fleeting meetings into lasting lessons.

- For every networking event or mentorship meeting, jot down who you met, key takeaways, and any follow-up actions you plan to take. This habit ensures valuable insights don't get lost in the shuffle of daily life.

- Reflect on these encounters. How do they align with your career goals? Is there wisdom shared that could pivot your path or strategy?

Career Visioning

Your career is more than a list of job titles and achievements; it's a narrative of growth, challenges, and aspirations. Through career visioning in your journal, you draft the chapters yet to be written, designing a roadmap to the future you envision.

- Dedicate pages to visualize your ideal professional life. Describe not just the roles you aim to fill but also the impact you want to have, the culture you wish to be part of, and the balance you seek between work and personal life.

- Break down this vision into actionable objectives. What can you do this year, this month, or even today to edge closer to that ideal?

In weaving journaling into the fabric of your career development, you craft a tool that's both mirror and map. It reflects where you stand today—your strengths, your challenges, your victories—and outlines the path to where you aspire to be. This practice is more than a habit; it's a commitment to continuous growth and self-discovery, ensuring that as you climb the ladder of your career, you remain rooted in your values, driven by your goals, and open to the journey's unfolding.

9.4 Advanced Sketching Techniques

Imagine your journal as a gallery of your own creation, where every page offers a new exhibit of your thoughts, feelings, and the world as you see it. Now, think about elevating this gallery to the next level with advanced sketching techniques. It's not just about making things look prettier; it's about adding layers of depth and meaning to your entries, transforming them into pieces that not only catch the eye but also speak to the soul.

Elevating Your Art

To elevate your art, you must first shake hands with a few advanced techniques that might seem daunting at first glance but are really just friends you haven't met yet. Perspective, shading, and figure drawing are the trio that will help you bring your sketches from flat to fully dimensional.

- **Perspective**: Start by playing with vanishing points on your pages. A simple hallway or a road stretching into the horizon can become an engaging study in perspective, adding depth to your visual storytelling.
- **Shading**: Experiment with light and shadow to give your objects form and weight. Notice where the light in your environment falls and try to replicate that in your sketches. This practice not only enhances the realism of your drawings but also adds a dramatic flair to your pages.
- **Figure Drawing**: Humans are complex, but breaking down the body into simple shapes can make figure drawing less intimidating. Practice sketching people in various poses, focusing on the flow of movement and the basic proportions. Over time, this practice will add life and movement to your journal entries.

Incorporating Multimedia Art

Your journal is a playground, and multimedia art is the sandbox where different elements come together. Here, sketching meets painting, collage, and even digital elements, creating dynamic entries that burst off the page.

- Start with a sketch, then layer watercolors over it for a dreamy effect. The watercolor can enhance the sketch, adding mood and atmosphere.
- Try adding collage elements. A sketch of a tree might be enhanced with leaves from a magazine or a printed photo of a forest as the background, creating a rich tapestry of textures.
- Digital elements, like printed photos or digital drawings, can also play a role. A digitally drawn bird could land on a hand-drawn tree, marrying the analog and digital worlds in your journal.

Sketching from Life

There's something magical about capturing the world as it unfolds around you. Sketching from life not only improves your observation skills but also adds authenticity and immediacy to your journal sketches. It's about seeing the beauty in everyday moments and translating that onto your pages.

- Carry your journal with you and take moments to sketch the world as you see it, whether it's a cup of coffee at your favorite café or the bustling street on your way to work. These sketches serve as windows into your daily life, making your journal a true reflection of your world.

- Don't worry about getting every detail perfect. The goal is to capture the essence of the moment, which often lies in the imperfections and the spontaneity of the sketch.

Art as Reflection

Your journal is more than just a collection of pretty pages; it's a mirror reflecting your inner world. Advanced sketching techniques can serve as tools for deeper self-expression and reflection, turning each entry into a dialogue with yourself.

- Use figure drawing to explore emotions. A series of sketches depicting different postures or expressions can be a powerful way to process and express feelings that are hard to put into words.

- Experiment with abstract sketches that reflect your mood or thoughts for the day. Sometimes, a swirl of lines and shapes can say more about your state of mind than a detailed drawing ever could.

In the end, these advanced sketching techniques are not just about making your journal more visually appealing; they're about enriching the storytelling within its pages. They allow you to capture the world with greater depth, express emotions with more nuance, and ultimately, create a journal that's as complex and layered as the life it documents. So, grab your pencil, and let's add some new dimensions to your journaling practice.

9.5 Digital Journaling Tools and Apps

In the tapestry of modern life, technology weaves intricate patterns, merging the timeless act of journaling with the boundless possibilities of the digital age. This fusion not only redefines our conception of a journal but also expands the horizon of our creative and reflective practices. Here, we explore the digital realm, discovering tools and apps that transform journaling from a solitary activity into a dynamic, multimedia experience.

Leveraging Technology

Navigating the digital landscape reveals a plethora of tools designed to enhance the journaling voyage. From apps that mimic the tactile feel of paper to platforms that secure our most private thoughts with cutting-edge encryption, technology offers something for every type of journaler.

- **Multimedia Integration**: Apps now enable the inclusion of photos, videos, and sound clips, turning journal entries into multimedia narratives. Imagine capturing the roar of a waterfall on a hiking trip or the serene silence of a sunrise, embedding these moments alongside your written reflections.
- Cloud Storage: The fear of losing a cherished journal dissipates with cloud storage, ensuring our memories and musings are safely archived and accessible from anywhere. This feature not only safeguards our entries but also liberates us from the physical constraints of traditional journaling.
- **Encryption and Privacy**: With concerns over digital privacy at an all-time high, many journaling apps offer encryption, requiring passwords or biometric verification. This layer of security provides peace of mind, allowing the free flow of thoughts without the worry of prying eyes.

Combining Digital and Analog

While the allure of digital journaling is undeniable, the charm of pen on paper remains unmatched. The key lies in harmonizing these two worlds, creating a journaling practice that captures the best of both.

- For moments that demand immediacy, digital tools stand ready. Quick thoughts jotted down on a smartphone can later be expanded upon within the pages of a physical journal.
- Transferring insights from digital to analog allows for deeper exploration. A photo captured on a phone can inspire a full-page watercolor illustration, or a voice memo can be transcribed and reflected upon in greater depth.

Digital Creativity

The digital realm opens up a playground of creative possibilities, where the constraints of the physical journal no longer bind us. Here, creativity knows no bounds, limited only by the expanse of our imagination.

- **Digital Collages**: Combining images, text, and graphics with drag-and-drop ease allows for the creation of complex visual narratives, blending the elements of traditional collage with digital efficiency.
- **Audio and Video Entries**: Sometimes, words fall short. Recording a voice note or video diary provides a dynamic alternative, capturing the nuance of emotion and the ambiance of the moment in a way that text alone cannot.

- **Digital Sketching and Painting**: With a stylus and tablet, the digital canvas becomes a realm for artistic exploration. Sketches and paintings created digitally can be more easily edited, shared, and integrated into journal entries, offering a new dimension to the visual aspect of journaling.

Privacy and Security

As we venture further into the digital journaling space, the sanctity of our personal reflections becomes a paramount concern. The digital age, while offering unparalleled possibilities, also presents unique challenges in safeguarding our privacy.

- When selecting a digital journaling platform, prioritize those offering robust encryption and privacy policies. Understanding how and where your data is stored can help in making an informed choice.
- Regularly update passwords and consider using a password manager to maintain the security of your digital journal. In a world where digital breaches are not uncommon, these practices are essential in protecting your personal reflections.

Navigating the intersection of traditional and digital journaling reveals a landscape rich with possibility. Here, the tactile pleasure of pen on paper meets the dynamic potential of multimedia, cloud storage brings peace of mind, and encryption ensures our innermost thoughts remain our own. In this digital age, our journals transform into living, breathing entities, chronicling our journeys with a vibrancy and depth that was once unimaginable. Through the thoughtful integration of digital tools and apps, we not only preserve our past but also illuminate the path forward, crafting a journaling practice that is as multifaceted and diverse as the lives we lead.

9.6 Creating a Journaling Blog or Vlog

Imagine transforming your personal journaling practice into a beacon of inspiration for others. Whether through the written word on a blog or the moving images of a vlog, sharing your journey opens up a world of connection, creativity, and community. This isn't just about broadcasting your life; it's about inviting others into a space where growth, reflection, and inspiration flourish. Below, discover how to weave your personal narratives into a shared tapestry that resonates with fellow journal enthusiasts and newcomers alike.

Sharing Your Journey

The first step is to consider the platform that best suits your style. Are you more comfortable writing detailed posts, or does the idea of speaking directly to an audience through video excite you? Both blogs and vlogs offer unique ways to share your journey, each with its own set of tools to bring your stories to life.

- For bloggers, platforms like WordPress or Blogger provide customizable spaces to craft your posts, embed images, and interact with your readers through comments.

- Vloggers might lean towards YouTube or Vimeo, where editing tools can help stitch together clips of your journaling process, reflections, or even live journaling sessions.

Content Ideas

The heart of your blog or vlog lies in the content you choose to share. Here, the breadth of your journaling practice offers endless inspiration. From the tactile thrill of flipping through your pages to the introspective moments that lead to breakthroughs, your content can serve as both a guide and a companion to those on their own journaling paths.

- **Journaling Tips and Techniques**: Share your favorite methods, tools, and hacks that have shaped your journaling practice. From choosing the right pen to mastering the art of bullet journaling, your insights can offer valuable guidance.

- **Prompt Challenges**: Engage your audience with creative prompt challenges. Invite them to explore themes or questions along with you, creating a shared journaling experience that spans the digital divide.

- **Thematic Entries**: Highlight entries centered around specific themes, such as gratitude, personal growth, or mindfulness. Discuss the impact these focused reflections have had on your life, encouraging others to explore similar paths.

- **Personal Growth Stories**: Perhaps the most powerful content comes from sharing your journey of growth and change. By opening up about the challenges you've faced, and the lessons learned, you create a space for genuine connection and inspiration.

Maintaining Privacy

While sharing your journey can be rewarding, it's essential to navigate the balance between openness and privacy. Your journal holds intimate reflections, and not every page is meant for public viewing. Here's how to share authentically while safeguarding your privacy:

- **Anonymize Sensitive Information**: Before sharing images of your journal or recounting personal stories, ensure you've removed or blurred out any sensitive information. This might include names, locations, or details that you prefer to keep private.

- **Selective Sharing**: Decide in advance which aspects of your journaling practice you're comfortable sharing publicly. You might choose to focus on the process and outcomes rather than the deeply personal content of your entries.

- **Content Warnings**: If you're discussing topics that might be triggering or sensitive for some audiences, including content warnings at the beginning of your posts or videos can foster a respectful and safe space for your viewers.

Building a Community

Perhaps the most rewarding aspect of sharing your journaling journey online is the opportunity to build a community. This isn't just about amassing followers; it's about fostering connections, sharing insights, and supporting each other's growth.

- **Engage with Your Audience**: Make it a priority to respond to comments, messages, and emails. Engagement fosters a sense of belonging and encourages an ongoing dialogue among your viewers or readers.
- **Collaborate with Other Creators**: Reach out to fellow journaling enthusiasts for guest posts, joint vlogs, or collaborative projects. These partnerships can introduce your audience to new perspectives and techniques, enriching the community as a whole.
- **Supportive Environment**: Cultivate a space where encouragement, respect, and constructive feedback are the norms. Your blog or vlog can become a haven for those seeking inspiration and a sense of connection in their journaling journey.

In sharing your journaling journey through blogging or vlogging, you open a window into a world where personal reflections become communal treasures. It's a space where stories unfold, ideas blossom, and connections deepen. By guiding others on their path, you not only illuminate the way but also discover new insights and inspirations for your own journey. Through careful crafting of content, mindful maintenance of privacy, and nurturing of community, your blog or vlog can grow into a vibrant, shared journaling adventure.

9.7 The Science of Journaling: Research and Studies

In the vast ocean of personal development and self-care, journaling stands out not just as a beacon of light but as a scientifically backed vessel steering us towards improved mental health, cognitive function, and emotional well-being. The body of research illuminating the benefits of journaling is both rich and expanding, offering fascinating insights into how this ancient practice can be a potent tool in our modern lives.

Evidence-Based Benefits

Diving into the scientific studies, one finds a treasure trove of evidence supporting the positive impact of journaling. Investigations have shown that regular journaling can act as a stress relief valve, helping to lower anxiety and reduce the physical symptoms associated with stress. Furthermore, the practice has been linked to enhanced immune function, with participants in one study experiencing fewer illness-related visits to the doctor following a period of expressive writing.

- Studies underscore journaling's role in boosting mood and providing a sense of emotional release, allowing individuals to process complex feelings and find meaning in challenging experiences.

- Cognitive benefits are also on the ledger, with research indicating that journaling can sharpen memory and comprehension by providing a space for reflection and critical thinking.

Journaling in Therapeutic Settings

The application of journaling extends into clinical settings, where therapists and counselors use expressive writing interventions to aid clients in navigating their emotional landscapes. Whether addressing trauma, depression, or everyday stress, journaling becomes a conduit for healing and self-discovery.

- Clinical trials have observed significant improvements in the mental health of participants who engaged in structured journaling exercises, highlighting its effectiveness as an adjunct to traditional therapy.
- In these therapeutic contexts, journaling acts not only as an outlet for emotional expression but also as a tool for problem-solving and coping strategy development, fostering resilience and personal growth.

Future Research Directions

The horizon of journaling research is broad and promising, with several areas ripe for exploration. As we deepen our understanding of the brain's response to expressive writing, future studies might illuminate how journaling contributes to neural plasticity and emotional regulation. Additionally, the integration of digital journaling tools and their impact on mental health presents a fascinating frontier for investigation.

- Investigating the long-term effects of journaling on mental health and well-being, particularly in diverse populations and age groups, could offer valuable insights into its therapeutic potential.
- With the rise of digital platforms, assessing the differences between traditional and digital journaling practices in terms of efficacy and user experience becomes an intriguing focus for future research.

Applying Research to Practice

Equipped with the knowledge that journaling is more than just a feel-good activity—it's a practice grounded in science—incorporating research findings into your journaling routine can enhance its benefits. Whether you're a seasoned journaler or new to the practice, consider these evidence-based approaches to maximize your journaling experience:

- Set aside dedicated time for expressive writing, especially during periods of stress or transition. Aim for uninterrupted sessions where you can delve deep into your thoughts and feelings.
- Experiment with different journaling formats, such as gratitude lists, free-writing, or reflective prompts, to discover which methods resonate most with you and yield the greatest emotional or cognitive benefits.
- Integrate journaling into your broader self-care or therapeutic regimen, using it as a tool to complement other practices such as mindfulness meditation, therapy, or physical exercise.

The science of journaling paints a compelling picture of its value as a multifaceted tool for enhancing our mental, emotional, and cognitive health. As research continues to unfold, it invites us to not only appreciate the depth of journaling's impact but also to weave its evidence-based practices into the fabric of our daily lives. Through this informed approach, journaling transcends its status as a mere activity, becoming a vital ally in our journey towards wellness and self-discovery.

9.8 Journaling for Educational Purposes

In the realm of education, the simple act of writing down thoughts and reflections transcends mere note-taking. It becomes a bridge connecting knowledge to understanding, information to insight. This section peels back the layers of journaling's role in educational settings, shining a light on its power to enhance learning and retention from the classroom to the library and beyond.

Learning Through Reflection

The quiet introspection that journaling encourages is not just beneficial; it's transformative. It allows students of all ages to pause and process the whirlwind of information encountered daily. This reflective practice is crucial in settings ranging from elementary classrooms to university lecture halls and even in the lifelong learning journeys of adults.

- Implement reflection journals after each lesson or module, prompting students to write about what they learned, questions they still have, and connections to their own lives or experiences.
- Encourage educators to model this practice, sharing their reflections on teaching methodologies or professional development experiences, thus fostering a culture of continuous learning and growth.

Study and Revision Journals

The journey from learning to mastery is paved with repetition and reflection. Study and revision journals serve as personalized textbooks, filled with the learner's summaries, interpretations, and questions. They transform passive study sessions into active engagements with the material.

- Suggest students create summary pages for each key concept or chapter, using their own words to distill the essence of the lessons. This practice not only aids retention but also makes revisiting topics before exams more efficient.
- Teach techniques like question-based reflection, where students formulate potential exam questions based on their understanding, and concept mapping, visually linking ideas and themes, to deepen comprehension and recall.

Journaling for Language Learning

The journey to fluency in a new language is both exhilarating and daunting. Journaling offers a sandbox for experimentation and practice, free from the fear of mistakes.

- Encourage daily entries in the target language, starting with simple sentences about the day's events and gradually incorporating new vocabulary and complex structures. This daily practice boosts comfort and confidence in written communication.

- Use journal entries as a space for cultural reflection, where learners can explore the customs, literature, and nuances of the cultures associated with the language they're studying, deepening their understanding and appreciation.

Integrating Journaling into Curricula

For educators aiming to weave journaling into their teaching tapestries, the question isn't why, but how. The versatility of journaling means it can complement any subject, enriching the curriculum and deepening students' engagement.

- In science classes, lab journals not only track experiments but also encourage students to hypothesize, observe, and reflect on the scientific process, fostering a hands-on understanding of scientific inquiry.

- In literature or history, character journals invite students to write from the perspective of historical figures or fictional characters, promoting empathy and a deeper connection to the material.

- For math, reflective journals might seem less intuitive but are equally valuable. Encouraging students to write about their problem-solving processes can unveil misconceptions and solidify strategies, making abstract concepts more concrete.

In each of these educational landscapes, journaling acts as a catalyst for deeper learning and engagement. It's a practice that respects the individuality of learners, adapting to fit their unique paths to understanding. Through journaling, education becomes not just a transfer of knowledge but a dialogue, a shared exploration of the world and our place within it.

9.9   Legacy Journaling for Future Generations

In the quiet moments spent with pen in hand, journaling transcends being a mere personal exercise, morphing into a treasure trove for those we might never meet. Crafting journals with an eye toward the future invites us to ponder not just on the ephemeral but on what endures, creating a legacy that speaks across generations. This is the essence of legacy journaling, a practice that intertwines the personal with the perpetual, ensuring that our stories, lessons, and reflections outlive us, offering guidance, inspiration, and connection to future readers.

Journaling with Posterity in Mind

The first step in legacy journaling involves shifting our perspective from the immediate to the infinite. It's about weaving narratives and insights that hold value beyond our present moment, crafting entries that serve as both mirror and map for those who come after us. This doesn't mean every entry must be profound; rather, it's about imbuing our reflections with a consciousness of their potential impact and resonance.

- When jotting down daily experiences, consider including context or background information that future readers might not be familiar with, turning personal anecdotes into historical snapshots.
- Reflect on and document the lessons learned from challenges and successes alike. These reflections become the wisdom passed down, invaluable for those navigating their own paths.

Choosing Timeless Topics

Certain themes possess a timeless quality, resonating as much with future generations as they do with us. Focusing on these universal themes ensures that the content of our journals remains relevant and engaging, no matter the era in which they're read.

- Explore and document your personal values and how they've shaped your decisions and life path. Values are the compass by which we navigate life, and sharing your compass offers direction to others.
- Life milestones, be they joyful or challenging, are landmarks of the human experience. Documenting your feelings, lessons learned, and insights gained during these times provides a rich narrative for future readers.
- Reflections on societal changes offer a window into the world as you experienced it. These entries can serve as a valuable historical record, providing context and depth to the understanding of an era.

Physical Preservation

Ensuring that our journals can withstand the test of time is a crucial aspect of legacy journaling. This involves not just the content of our writings but the physical medium itself.

- Opt for archival-quality paper, which is acid-free and designed to last for centuries without deteriorating. This choice is fundamental in preserving the integrity of your words.
- Consider your writing instrument carefully. Archival pens with ink that doesn't fade or bleed through paper are essential in maintaining the legibility of your entries.
- Storage plays a significant role in preservation. Keeping your journals in a cool, dry place, away from direct sunlight, helps prevent damage. Consider protective boxes or sleeves that can shield your journals from physical harm.

Digital Archiving

In our digital age, creating a digital counterpart to our physical journals ensures that our legacy can be preserved, shared, and accessed across the globe. Digital archiving involves scanning or typing out handwritten pages, creating a virtual copy that carries the essence of our analog efforts into the digital realm.

- Scanning your journals page by page can be a meticulous process, but it safeguards against the loss of physical copies. High-resolution scans capture not just the text but the nuance of your handwriting, doodles, and any ephemera included in your pages.

- For those who journal digitally from the start, backing up your entries in multiple locations—cloud storage, external hard drives, or even dedicated archival websites—ensures that your digital legacy is safe from technological mishaps.

- Consider the format of your digital archives. PDFs are widely accessible and durable digital formats, making them a suitable choice for preserving the layout and content of your pages.

In embracing the practice of legacy journaling, we bridge the gap between past, present, and future, crafting journals that serve not just as personal sanctuaries but as beacons for those we leave behind. This mindful approach to journaling imbues our pages with a sense of purpose and permanence, ensuring that our stories, reflections, and lessons become part of a larger, enduring narrative. Through the thoughtful selection of topics, careful preservation of our journals, and embracing digital archiving, we lay the groundwork for a legacy that transcends time, offering wisdom, insight, and connection to future generations on their journeys through life.

9.10 The Philosophy Behind Journaling

In the gentle act of journaling, we weave a tapestry of thoughts and experiences, crafting a narrative that extends beyond the mere recounting of events. This practice, rooted in the depths of introspection and reflection, invites us to explore the philosophical underpinnings that give journaling its transformative power. Through the lens of philosophy, journaling becomes not just a method of recording life but a means of understanding it, questioning its essence, and contemplating our place within its vast expanse.

Exploring Journaling Philosophies

At its core, journaling serves as a bridge between the self and the universe, offering a space where the mundane meets the profound. Different philosophical perspectives view journaling as a spectrum of practices, from a meditative tool fostering mindfulness and presence to a vessel for existential exploration, probing questions of identity, purpose, and the very fabric of reality. These perspectives enrich our understanding of journaling, elevating it from a simple diary to a philosophical endeavor that challenges, nurtures, and transforms.

- Consider journaling as a mirror reflecting the self, an intimate conversation that reveals inner truths and fosters self-awareness.
- View journaling as a garden, where ideas are planted, nurtured, and harvested, contributing to personal growth and understanding.

Philosophical Journaling Prompts

To infuse your journaling practice with a deeper sense of philosophical inquiry, engage with prompts that challenge you to reflect on the bigger questions life poses. These prompts invite you to ponder your beliefs, examine your values, and explore the essence of your being, encouraging a journaling practice that is as enriching as it is introspective.

- What does happiness mean to me, and how do I pursue it in my daily life?
- Reflect on a moment of significant change. How did it shape your understanding of identity and the self?
- Contemplate the concept of time. How does your perception of the past, present, and future influence the way you live?
- Consider the role of solitude in your life. What have you discovered about yourself in moments of solitude?

Integrating Philosophy into Practice

Bringing philosophical concepts into your daily journaling enriches your entries with depth and nuance. This integration transforms your journal into a canvas where thoughts, musings, and reflections are painted with the broad strokes of inquiry and the fine lines of introspection.

- Start your journaling session with a moment of mindfulness, centering yourself in the present before delving into reflection.
- Use your journal as a space to explore ethical dilemmas or moral questions, writing about personal experiences that have challenged your values and beliefs.
- Dedicate pages to exploring concepts such as gratitude, impermanence, or connection, drawing from philosophical texts or your own insights.
- Create a "philosopher's corner" in your journal, a dedicated space for quotes, thoughts, and questions that spark deeper contemplation and exploration.

Reflecting on the Meaning of Journaling

As you journey through the pages of your journal, take time to reflect on what this practice means to you. How does it align with your search for meaning, your quest for understanding, and your exploration of the self? Journaling, in its essence, is a dialogue with the soul, a dance of words and thoughts that transcends the boundaries of the page and touches the heart of our existence.

- Ponder the role journaling plays in your life. Is it a sanctuary, a workshop, a gallery, or perhaps all three?
- Reflect on how your journaling practice has evolved. What have you learned about yourself, and how has your perspective on life shifted?
- Contemplate the legacy of your journal. What stories, insights, and wisdom do you hope to pass on through your words?

As we wrap up this exploration of the philosophical dimensions of journaling, we're reminded of the practice's profound ability to serve as a compass guiding us through the labyrinth of life. It's a tool for navigation, a light in the darkness, and a friend on the journey, offering solace, wisdom, and insight. As we turn the page, let us carry forward the lessons learned, the questions raised, and the reflections pondered, weaving them into the fabric of our lives and our ongoing narrative. In the chapters that lie ahead, may we continue to find depth, meaning, and understanding in the simple yet profound act of putting pen to paper.

Conclusion

Oh, what a ride it has been, my fellow journaling journeymen and journeywomen! From those shaky first lines, akin to a baby deer's first steps, to the majestic strides of a journaling unicorn, you've traversed the vast landscapes of self-expression, self-discovery, and, let's not forget, a healthy dose of self-amusement.

Remember the days when the thought of filling a blank page felt like being asked to climb Mount Everest in flip-flops? Look at you now, wielding your pen (or keyboard) like a knight of old wielded their sword, ready to conquer the dragons of doubt and the ogres of overwhelm. The transformative journey of journaling has, without a shadow of a doubt, turned you from a novice scribbler into a veritable maestro of musings, showcasing the incredible power journaling holds in corralling those wild, wandering thoughts and channeling them into streams of clarity, purpose, and oh-so-gratifying personal growth.

I cannot stress enough (and believe me, I've tried, even talking to my plants about it) the importance of making this wondrous practice a staple in your daily smorgasbord of activities. Like adding cheese to...well, anything, really - it just makes life better. Incorporating journaling into your daily routine is paramount for achieving that chef's kiss of mental clarity, creativity, and the delightful journey of self-discovery.

We've skipped and occasionally tripped through a kaleidoscope of journaling techniques and methods - from the life-altering Integrative Journaling (yes, it's a thing) to the joy-sparking KonMari method in journaling (Marie Kondo would be proud), not to mention the digital wizardry of journaling tools and the timeless treasure of legacy journaling. Each technique, a brushstroke contributing to the masterpiece that is your personalized journaling practice, highlighting the sheer versatility and adaptability of journaling to fit your unique, fabulous self.

Let's not forget the reason many of us turned to journaling in the first place - the quest for mental serenity. The therapeutic aspects of journaling have been like a balm for our bustling brains, helping manage the jitterbugs of anxiety, navigate the murky waters of depression, and foster a garden of positive mindset through gratitude journaling. It's the self-care routine we didn't know we needed but now can't live without.

Now, I'm nudging you (gently, with encouragement and possibly with a virtual slice of cake) to venture beyond the comfort of the familiar. Explore the vast expanse of advanced journaling techniques. Dabble in the digital, create a blog or vlog to share your journey, or dive deep into the science and philosophy that underpin this practice. There's a whole world out there in the journaling cosmos waiting to be discovered.

And as you embark on this ongoing adventure, tailor your journaling practice with the insights, techniques, and, let's not forget, the personal flair we've shared. Find what resonates with your soul, aligns with your goals, and fits snugly into your life like that favorite pair of socks on a cold morning.

Consider this not just a call to action but a call to continuous growth, to community engagement, and to sharing the boundless joys of journaling. The journaling community is a tapestry woven from the threads of individual experiences, learnings, and creations – your contributions add color, texture, and depth, enriching us all.

From the bottom of my ink-stained heart, thank you for joining me on this incredible journey. Your courage to explore, to express, and to grow through journaling is a beacon of inspiration. Keep that flame burning bright, my friends, and know that the best is yet to come.

And now, for one last nudge (picture me handing you a beautifully wrapped gift, but instead of a bow, it's got a quirky pen on top), I leave you with this reflective prompt: As you gaze upon the horizon of your journaling journey ahead, what impact do you envision it having on your life? What legacy do you wish to weave through the tapestry of your words and art?

May your pages be many, your ink flow freely, and your journey be ever joyous. Here's to the stories we tell and the lives we touch, one word at a time. Cheers!

Thank you for purchasing this book. If you have found it helpful, please go to Amazon and write a brief review. This would be so appreciated and will give others an idea of what this book is all about.

And please be looking for other books in this series that we will be publishing in the very near future.

Your input will be most appreciated.
Nick and Nora

References

- *Efficacy of journaling in the management of mental illness* https://www.ncbi.nlm.nih.gov/pmc/articles/PMC8935176/
- *How to Start Journaling: 7 Tips & Techniques for Beginners* https://www.betterup.com/blog/how-to-start-journaling
- *14 Life-Changing Journaling Techniques (And How To Start)* https://vanillapapers.net/2020/08/25/journaling-techniques/
- *The Impact of Gratitude on Mental Health* https://namica.org/blog/the-impact-of-gratitude-on-mental-health/
- *5 Ways to Bullet Journal to Benefit Your Mental Health* https://bulletjournal.com/blogs/bulletjournalist/5-ways-to-bullet-journal-to-benefit-your-mental-health
- *How To Start An Art Journal: A Complete Beginner's Guide* https://artfulhaven.com/how-to-start-an-art-journal/
- *Urban Nature Journaling: 7 Days of Artistic Prompts* https://learn.rosaliehaizlett.com/courses/urban-nature-journaling
- *Get Started – Zentangle* https://zentangle.com/pages/get-started
- *Why everyone should keep a journal — 7 surprising benefits* https://healthy.kaiserpermanente.org/health-wellness/healtharticle.7-benefits-of-keeping-a-journal
- *How to Build a Journaling Habit that Lasts* https://dayoneapp.com/blog/journaling-habit/
- *550+ Journal Prompts: The Ultimate List* https://dayoneapp.com/blog/journal-prompts/
- *Journaling for Personal Growth: The Impact of …* https://www.rosebud.app/blog/journaling-for-personal-growth
- *Color Psychology: How Color Affects Your Emotions And …* https://www.scienceofpeople.com/color-psychology/
- *To Draw Nature, Pick Up a Pencil and Really Look* https://www.nytimes.com/2021/05/09/at-home/draw-nature.html
- *Poetry as a Form of Self-Expression - Poems Please* https://poemsplease.com/poetry-as-a-form-of-self-expression/
- *The benefits of stream of consciousness writing* https://www.lifecoach-directory.org.uk/memberarticles/evoking-a-great-sense-of-release-the-benefits-of-stream-of-consciousness-writing
- *Sustained nature journaling can have positive educational …* https://nabt.org/files/galleries/ABT_Online_April_2023.pdf
- *Finding Urban Nature* https://www.nationalgeographic.org/idea/finding-urban-nature/

References

- *How To Start A Nature Journal - A Beginners Guide* https://www.lilyandthistle.com/how-to-start-a-nature-journal-today/
- *Mindfulness Activities, Exercises for Groups | 7 Nature Ideas* https://healingforest.org/2020/11/27/mindfulness-activities-exercises-groups/
- *Why We Should Embrace Mistakes in School* https://greatergood.berkeley.edu/article/item/why_we_should_embrace_mistakes_in_school
- *4 Effortless Ways to Integrate Journaling into your Life* https://kristinwise.com/blog-journaling/
- *500 Writing Prompts to Help Beat Writer's Block* https://www.writtenwordmedia.com/500-writing-prompts-to-help-beat-writers-doubt/
- *How Making Art Helps Improve Mental Health | Science* https://www.smithsonianmag.com/science-nature/can-art-therapy-help-patients-deal-with-mental-health-struggles-during-the-pandemic-180980310/
- *Positive Daily Affirmations: Is There Science Behind It?* https://positivepsychology.com/daily-affirmations/
- *Journaling for Anxiety Relief* https://www.verywellmind.com/journaling-a-great-tool-for-coping-with-anxiety-3144672
- *How Gratitude Changes You and Your Brain* https://greatergood.berkeley.edu/article/item/how_gratitude_changes_you_and_your_brain
- *The Effects of Bedtime Writing on Difficulty Falling Asleep* https://www.ncbi.nlm.nih.gov/pmc/articles/PMC5758411/
- *50 Visual Journal Prompts to Promote Drawing and Creative Thinking Skills* https://theartofeducation.edu/2018/04/50-visual-journal-prompts-to-promote-drawing-and-creative-thinking-skills/
- *The Ultimate Guide for Calligraphy Beginners* https://thepostmansknock.com/calligraphy-101-the-ultimate-guide-for-calligraphy-beginners/
- *Color Psychology in Art and Design - Linearity* https://www.linearity.io/blog/color-psychology/
- *Tips to Incorporate and Plan the Perfect Art Nature Lessons* https://theartofeducation.edu/2023/05/may-tips-to-incorporate-and-plan-the-perfect-art-nature-lessons/
- *What is Mixed Media Art Journaling - ZenGlyph* https://zenglyph.com/what-is-mixed-media-art-journaling/#:~:text=The%20purpose%20of%20mixed%20media%20art%20is%20to%20express%20yourself,creative%20expressions%20with%20no%20limits.
- *Home Page – KonMari | The Official Website of Marie Kondo* https://konmari.com/
- *The 7 best journal apps* https://zapier.com/blog/best-journaling-apps/
- *Supporting children's thinking and cognition through the visual arts* https://theeducationhub.org.nz/supporting-childrens-thinking-and-cognition-through-the-visual-arts/

Made in the USA
Middletown, DE
05 October 2018